Riverland

Lina Asfour-Muir

Copyright © 2025 Lina Asfour-Muir

All rights reserved. No part of this publication may be reproduced, distributed, or transmitted in any form or by any means, including photocopying, recording, or other electronic or mechanical methods, without the prior written permission of the publisher, except in the case of brief quotations embodied in critical reviews and certain other noncommercial uses permitted by copyright law.

For permission requests, contact lasfourmuir@gmail.com

ISBN: 978-1-997744-10-8

Published by: Windsor Press

Graphic Design by Louise Casavant

Riverland is a meditation on the fragile ecologies of the river near where I live—a place that has, for now, escaped the stains of unchecked development. Through submerged photographs, surface reflections, flower scans, and cyanotypes, the work traces the hidden and visible worlds that flourish here: the underworld beneath the water's surface, the delicate blooms along its banks, and the shifting play of light and shadow in ever-changing hues.

At its heart lies a question: *Can these untouched worlds endure?* As environmental degradation and relentless expansion press ever closer on the river's edge, the river becomes both sanctuary and warning. These images hold moments of stillness and fragility, asking what will remain if such places are lost.

Lina Asfour-Muir

Gatherings

Scanned flowers and leaves become fragments of the river's edge—small, intimate witnesses to its cycles. Isolated from their environment yet glowing with detail, they speak to a vitality that resides not only in grand landscapes but also in the fragile lives that grow quietly along the banks.

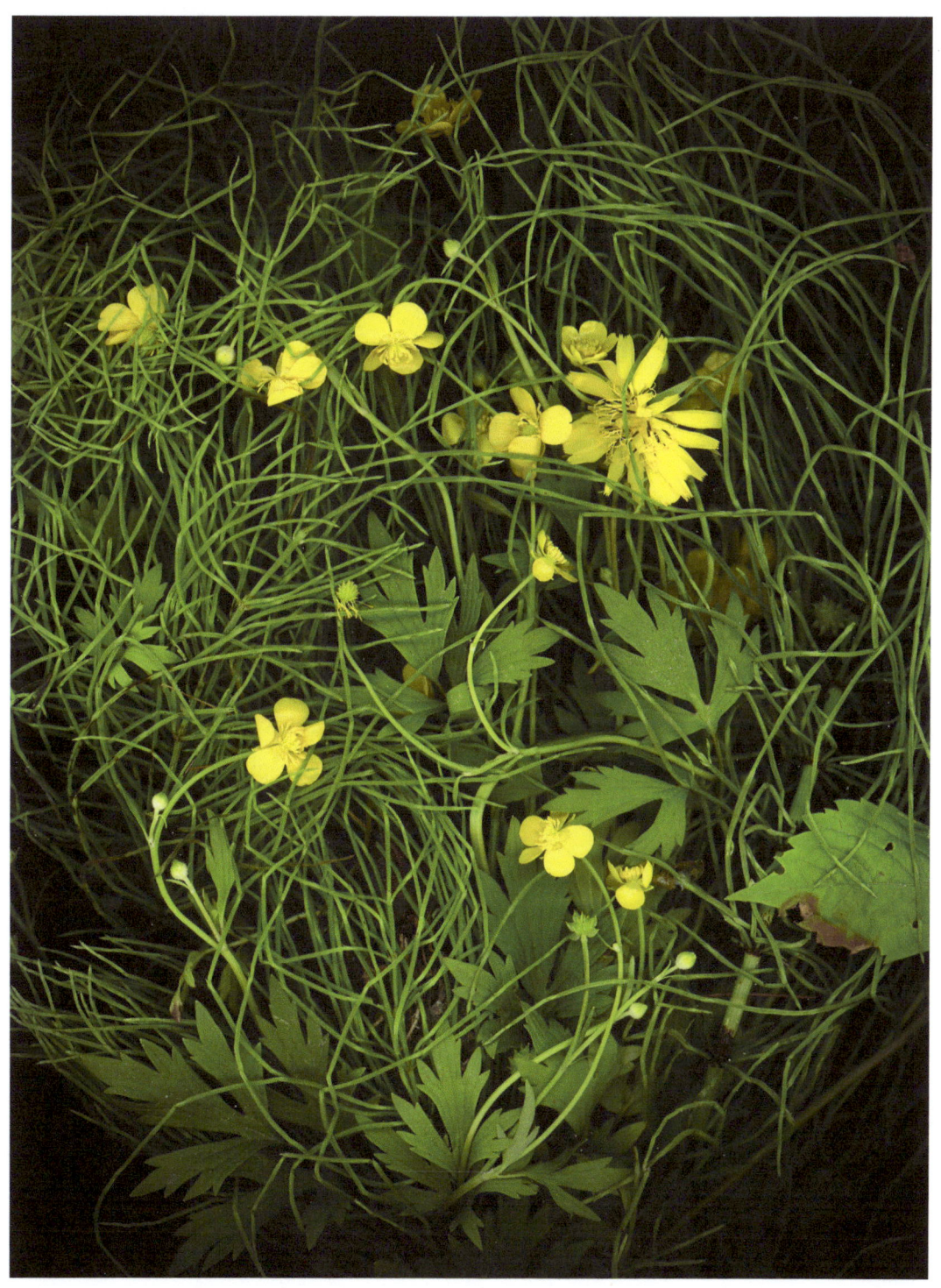

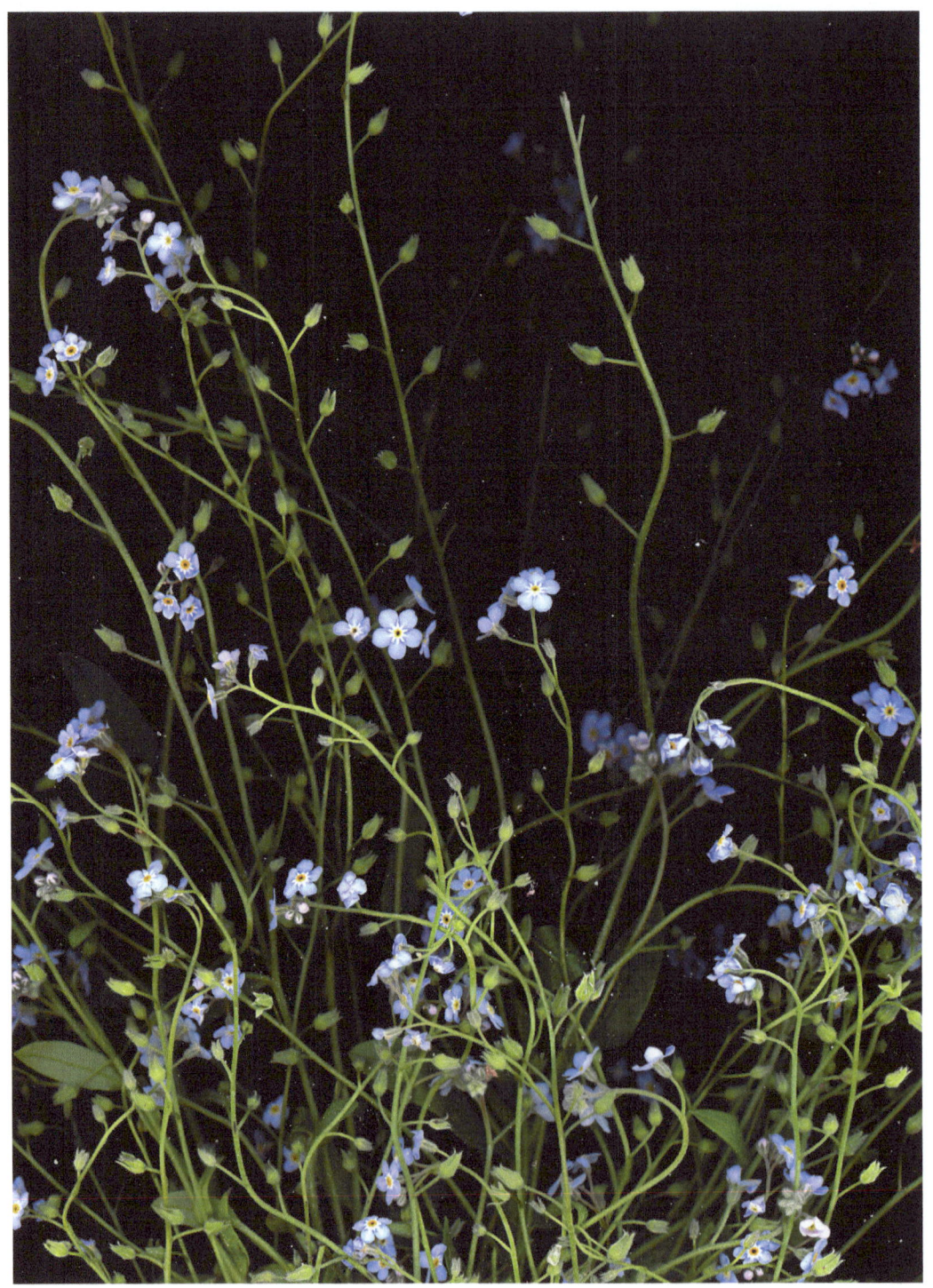

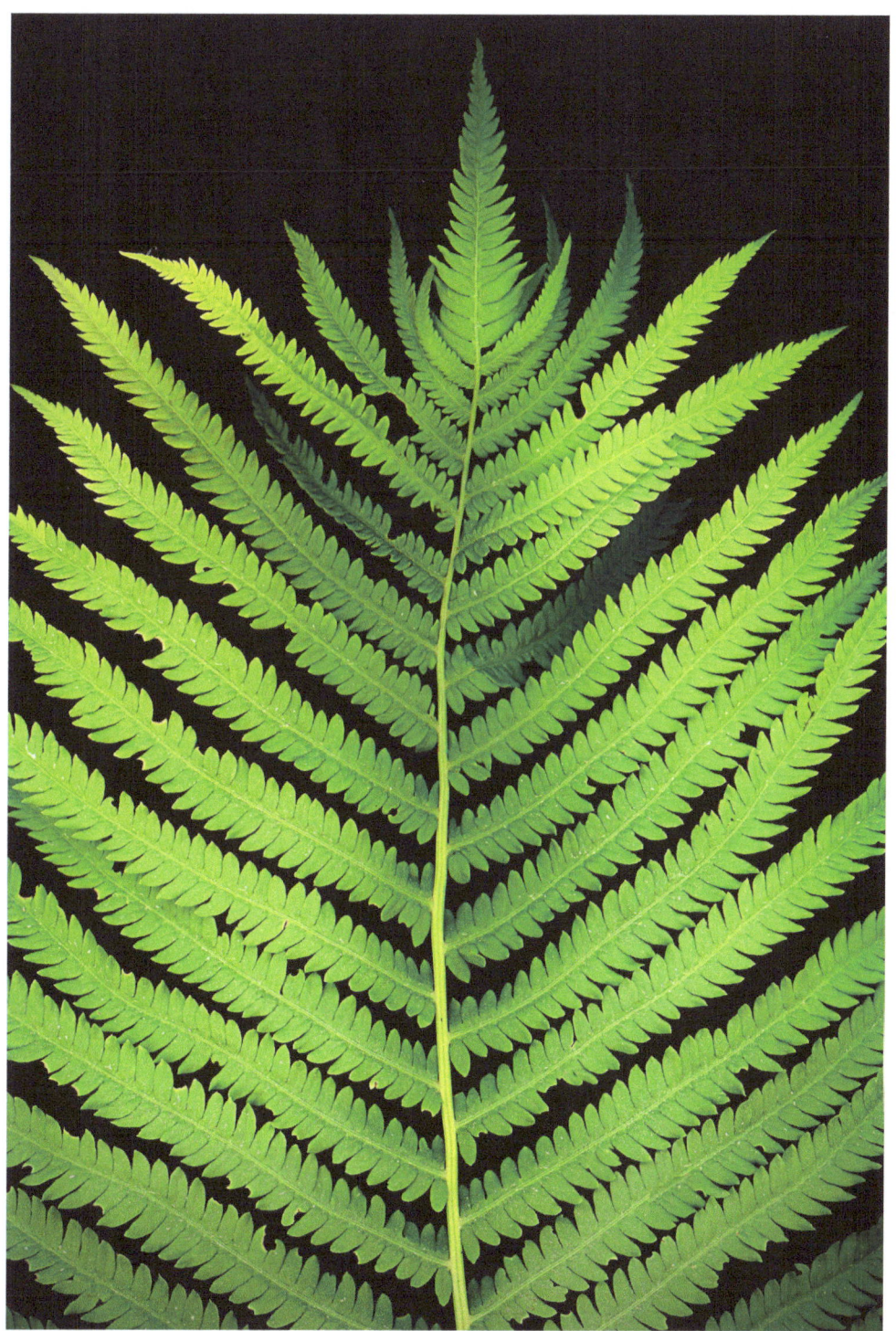

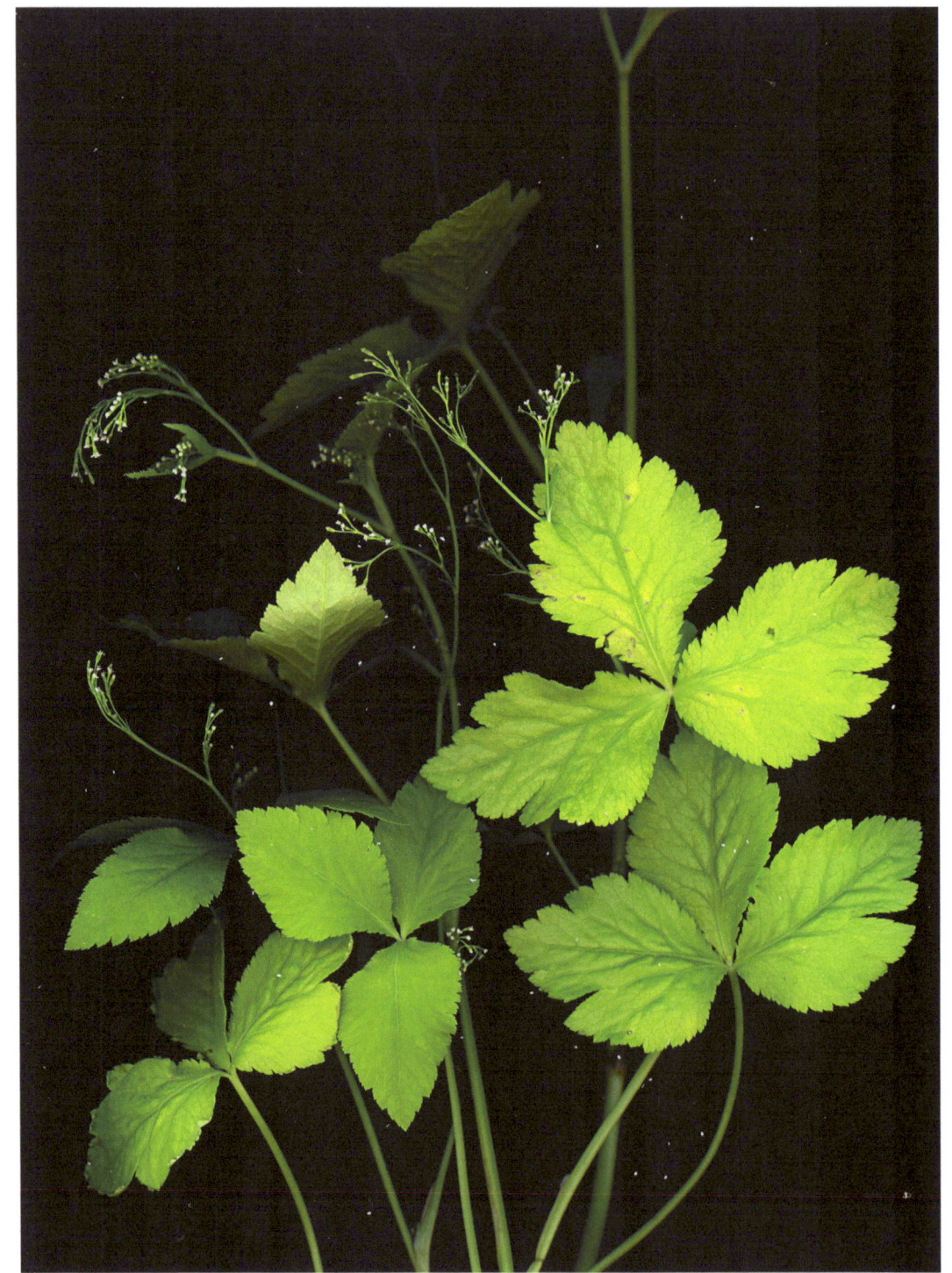

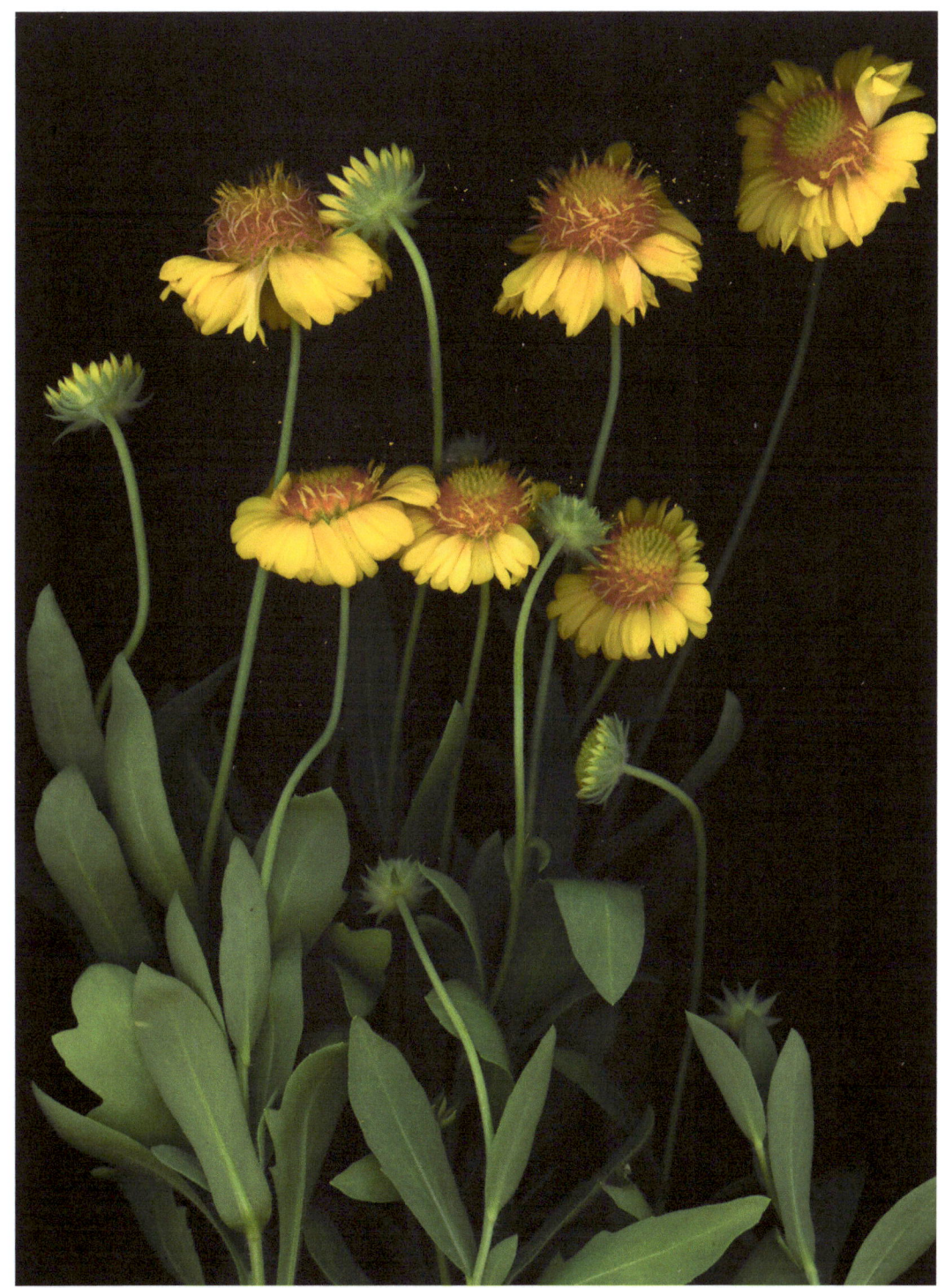

At the Surface

The river's journey begins in light. Familiar forms appear: grassy banks beneath wide skies, stems drifting into the shallows. Even here, there is a pull downward—hints of another vibrant world just below. This balance of land and water becomes an opening into the depths.

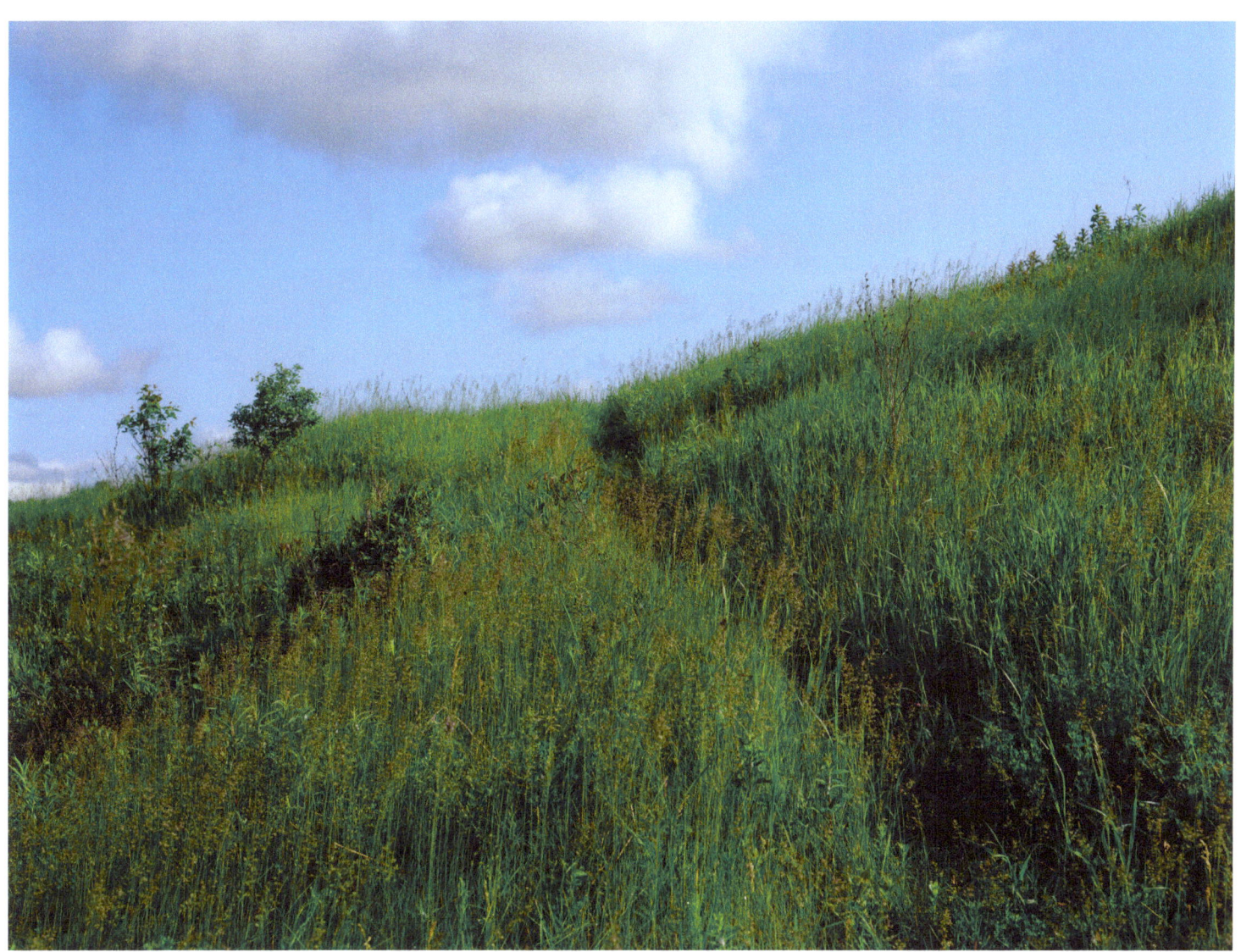

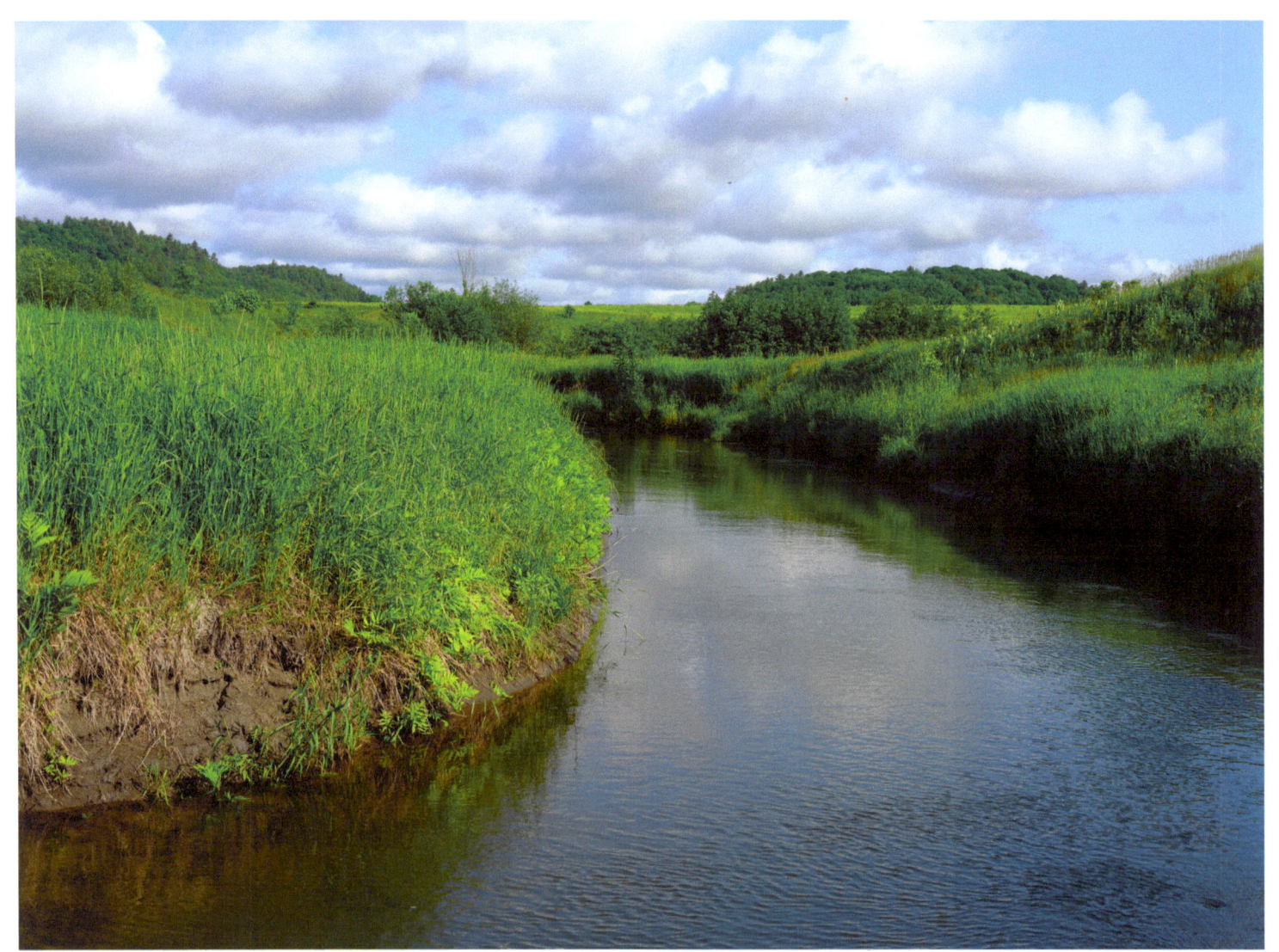

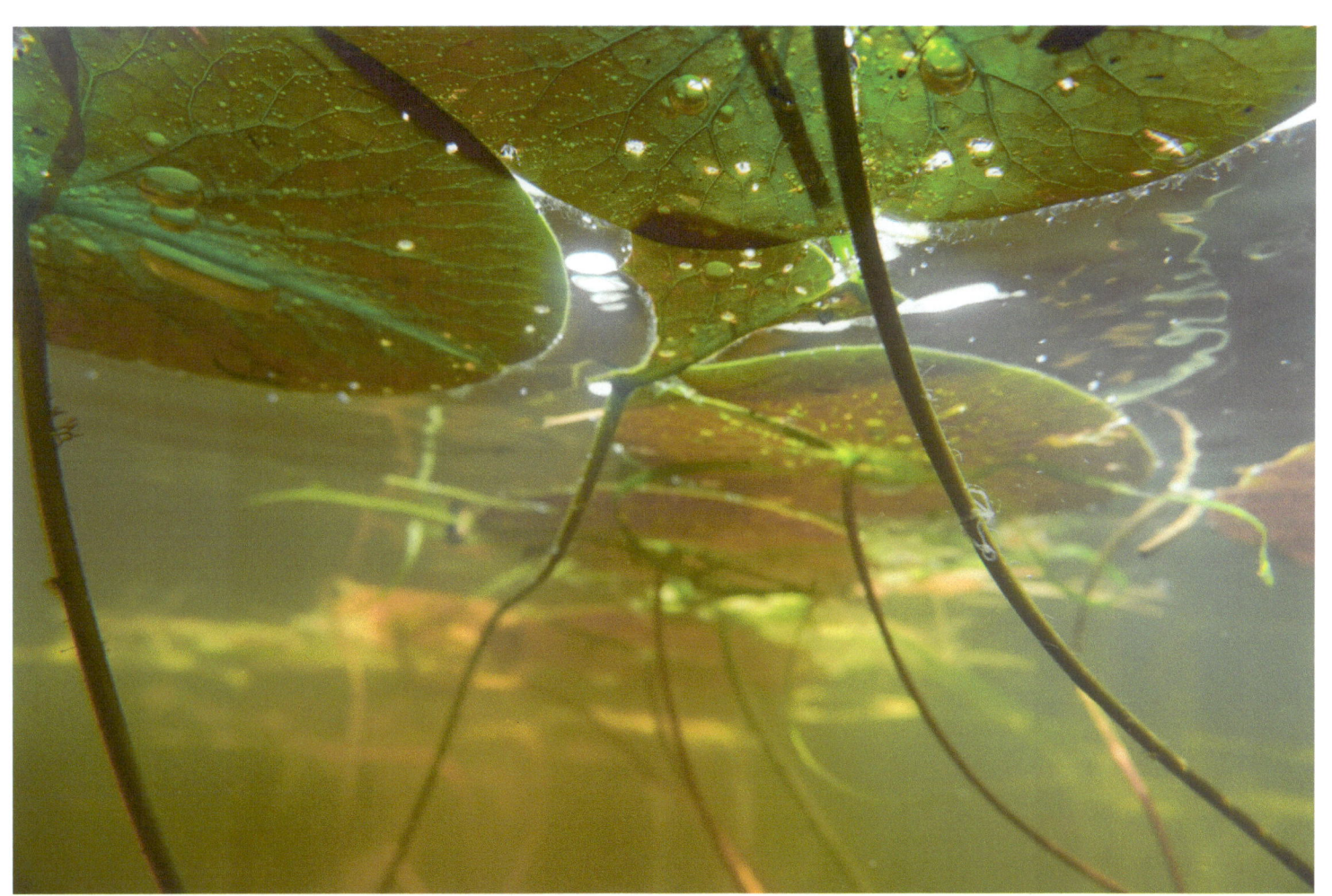

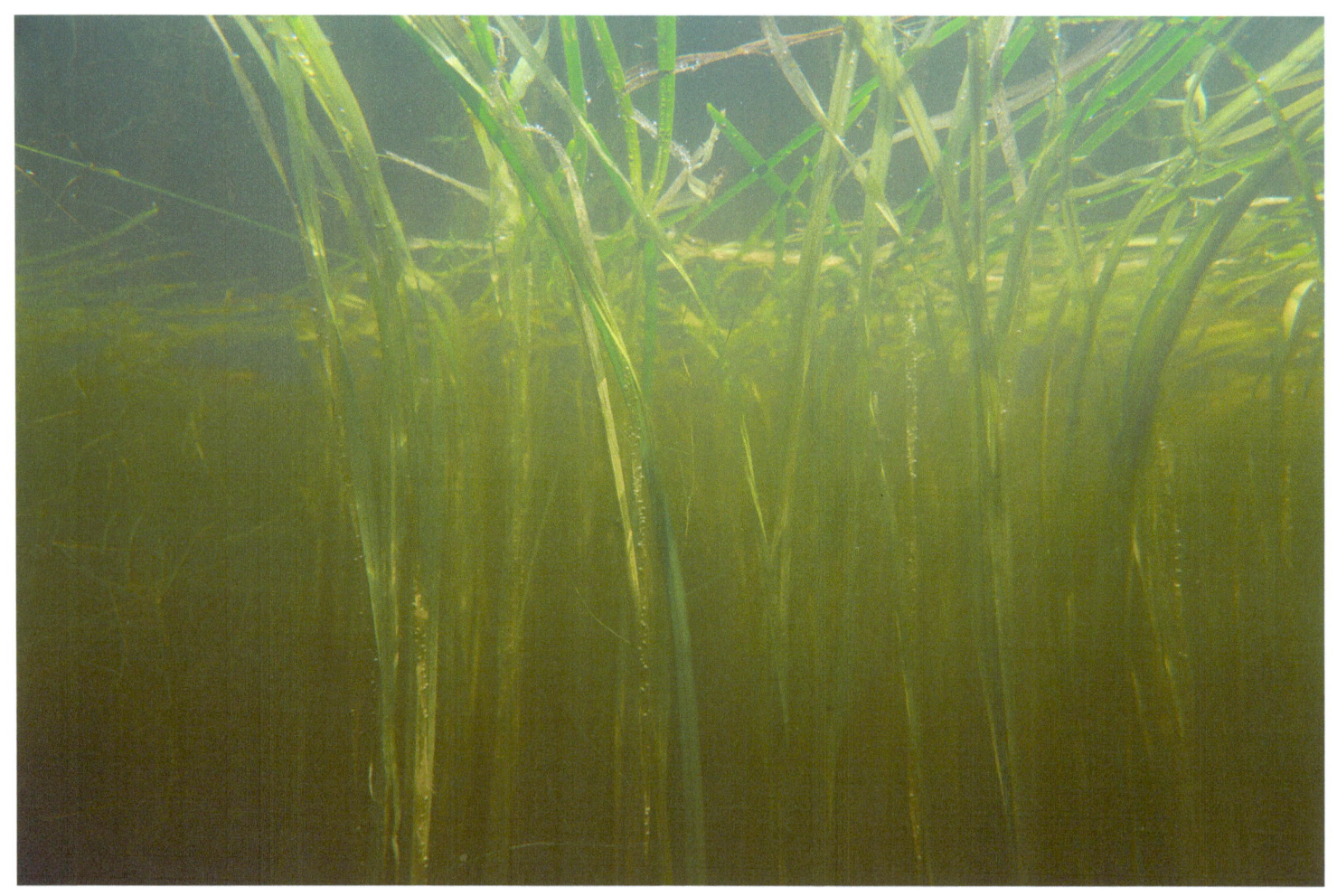

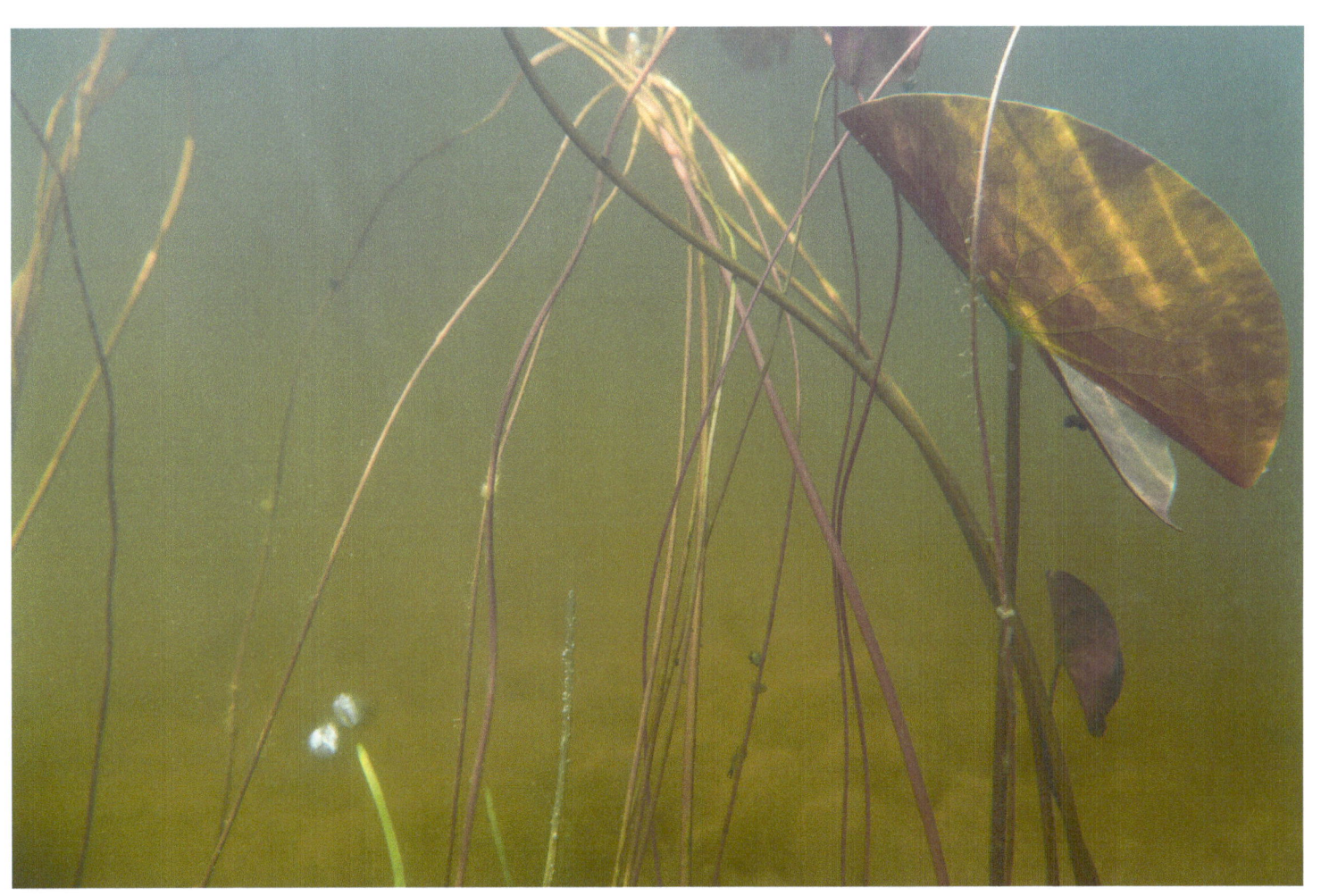

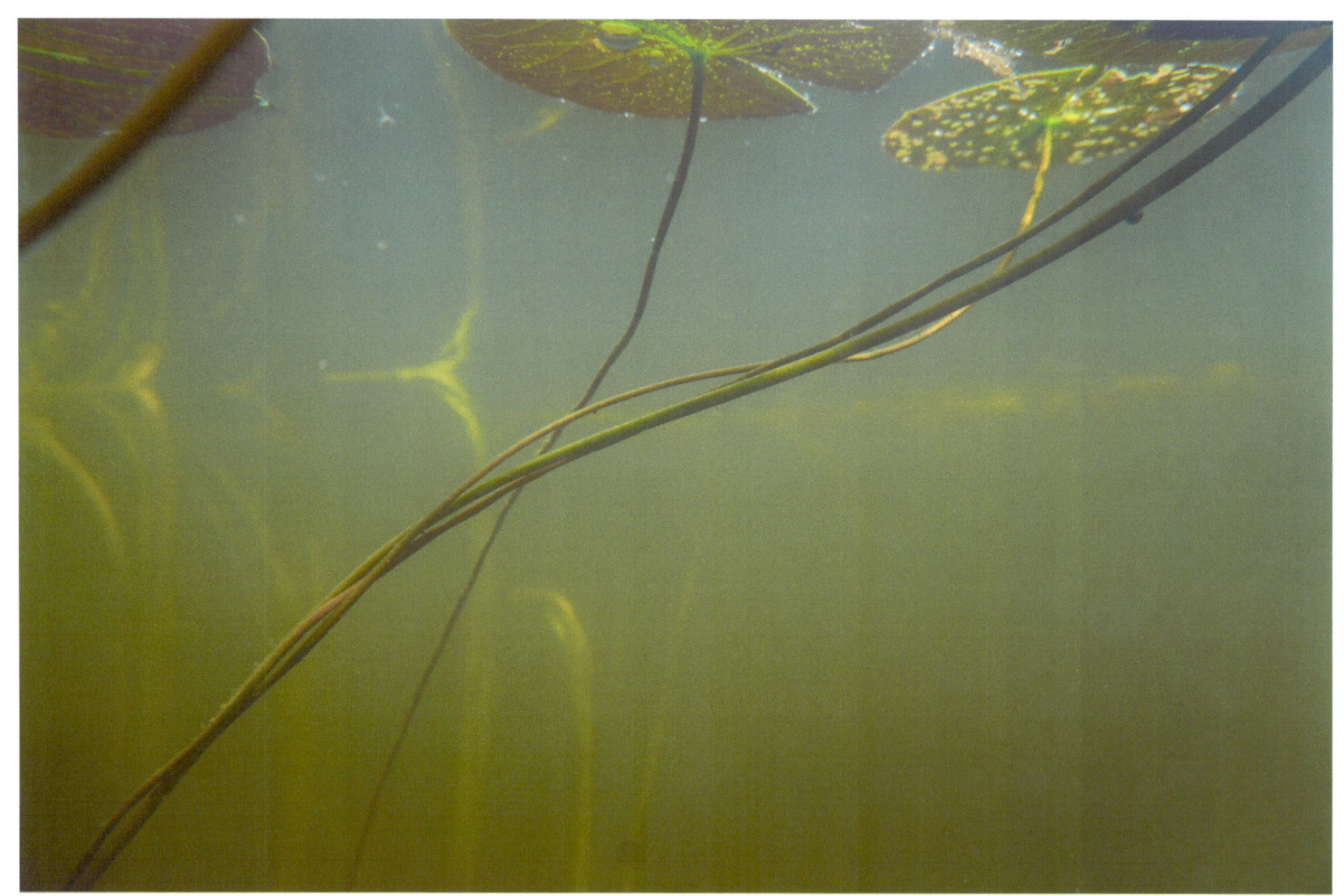

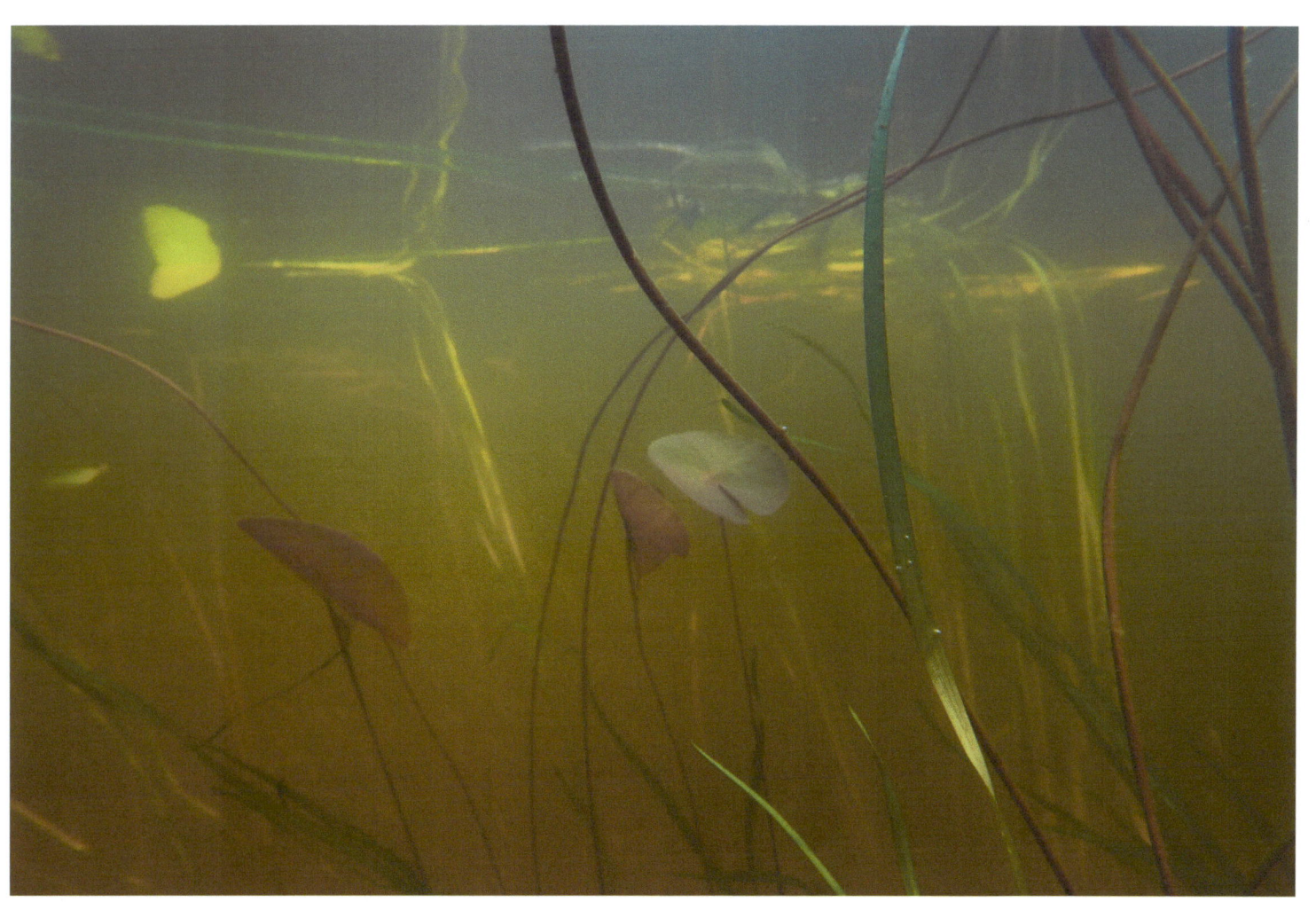

Beneath the Surface

Submerged in golden-red-brown waters, lilies stretch upward toward air, and light splinters across suspended stems. This is the river's hidden architecture, a hushed forest that thrives beyond human reach. The lens descends to capture the threshold where air meets water, where light bends and life persists quietly, unseen.

Not all depths glow in shadowed reds. In places, light refracts into luminous greens and yellows—tones that suggest renewal and movement toward the surface. Within these shifting palettes, the river reveals its multiplicity, many worlds flowing together beneath a single current.

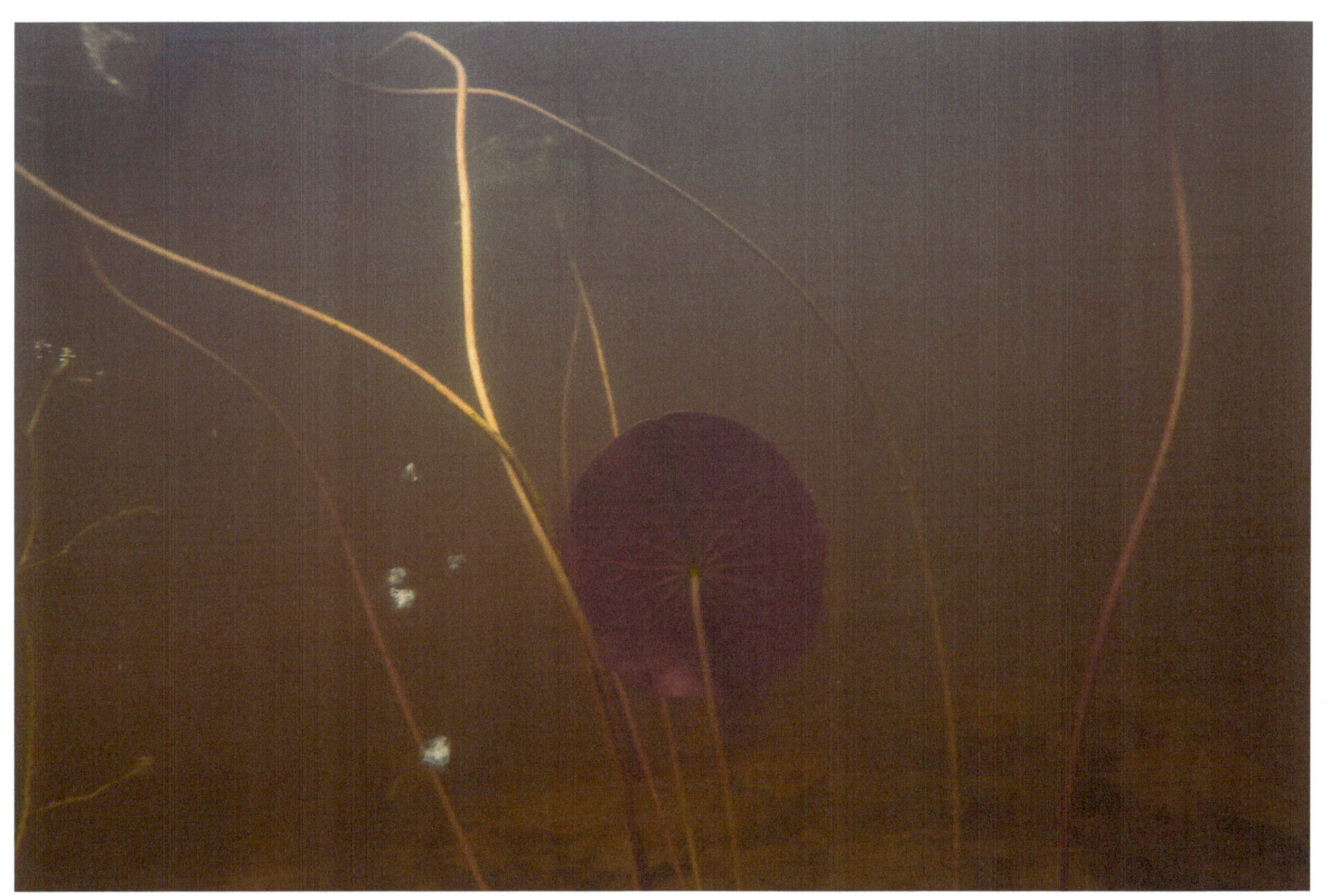

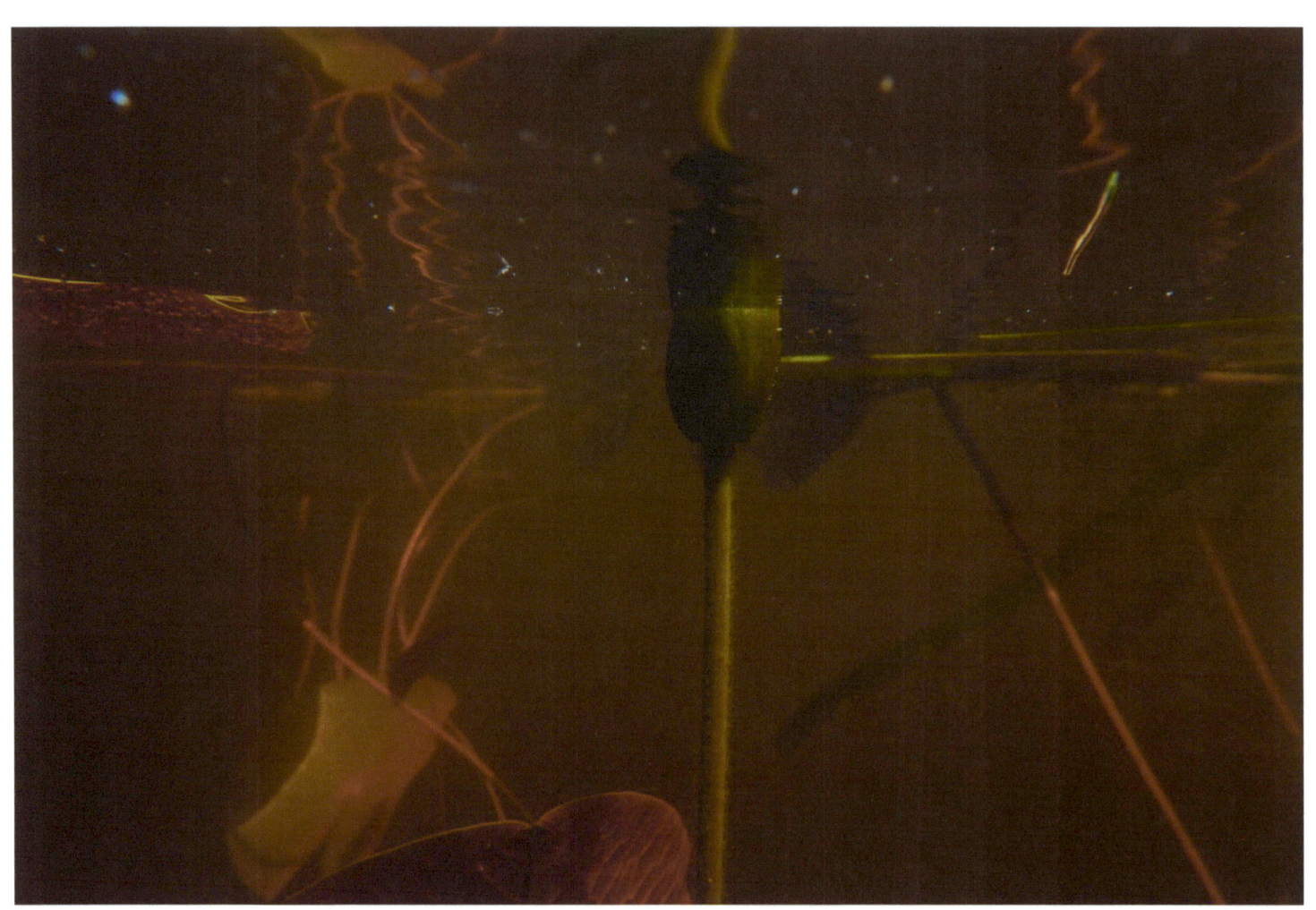

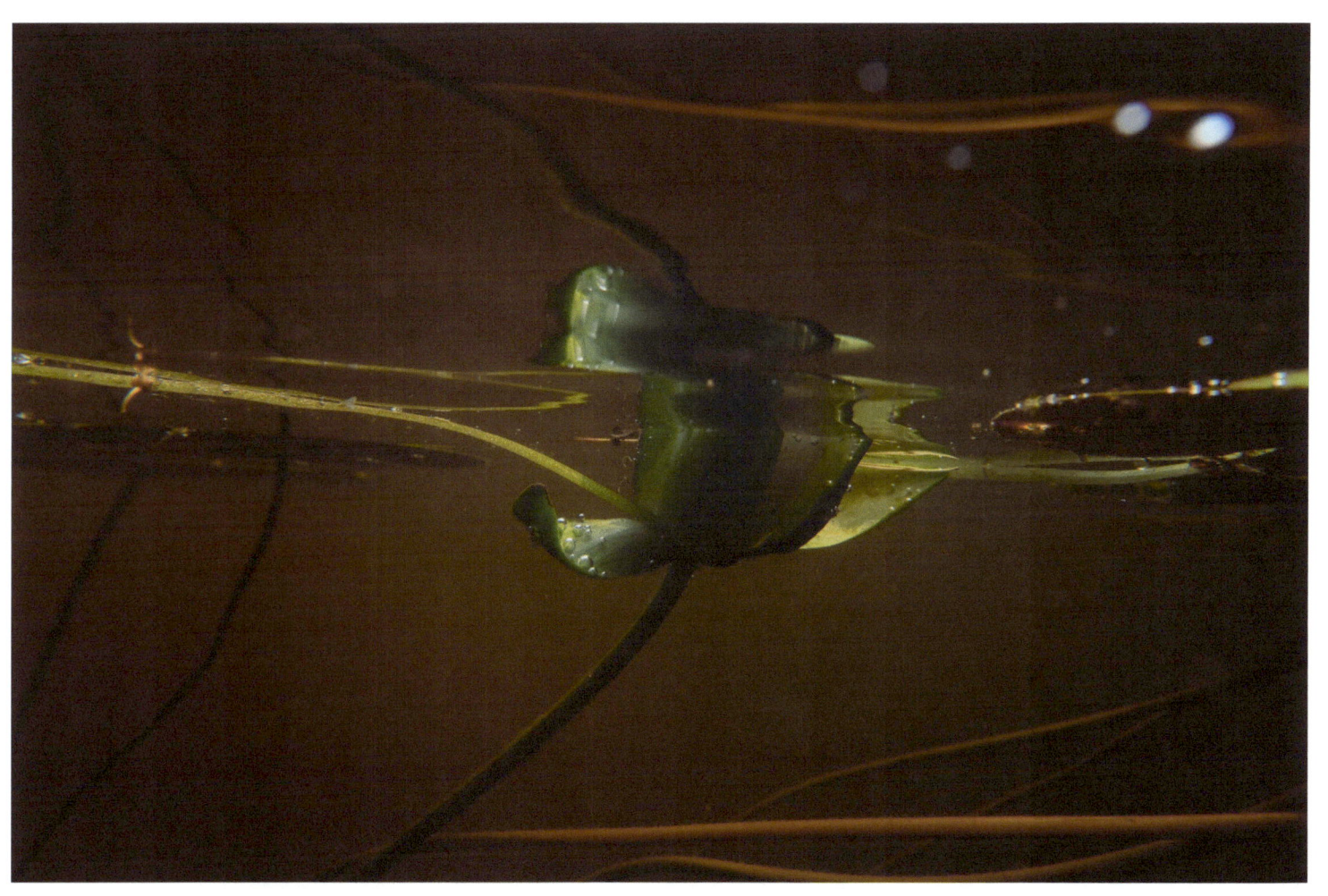

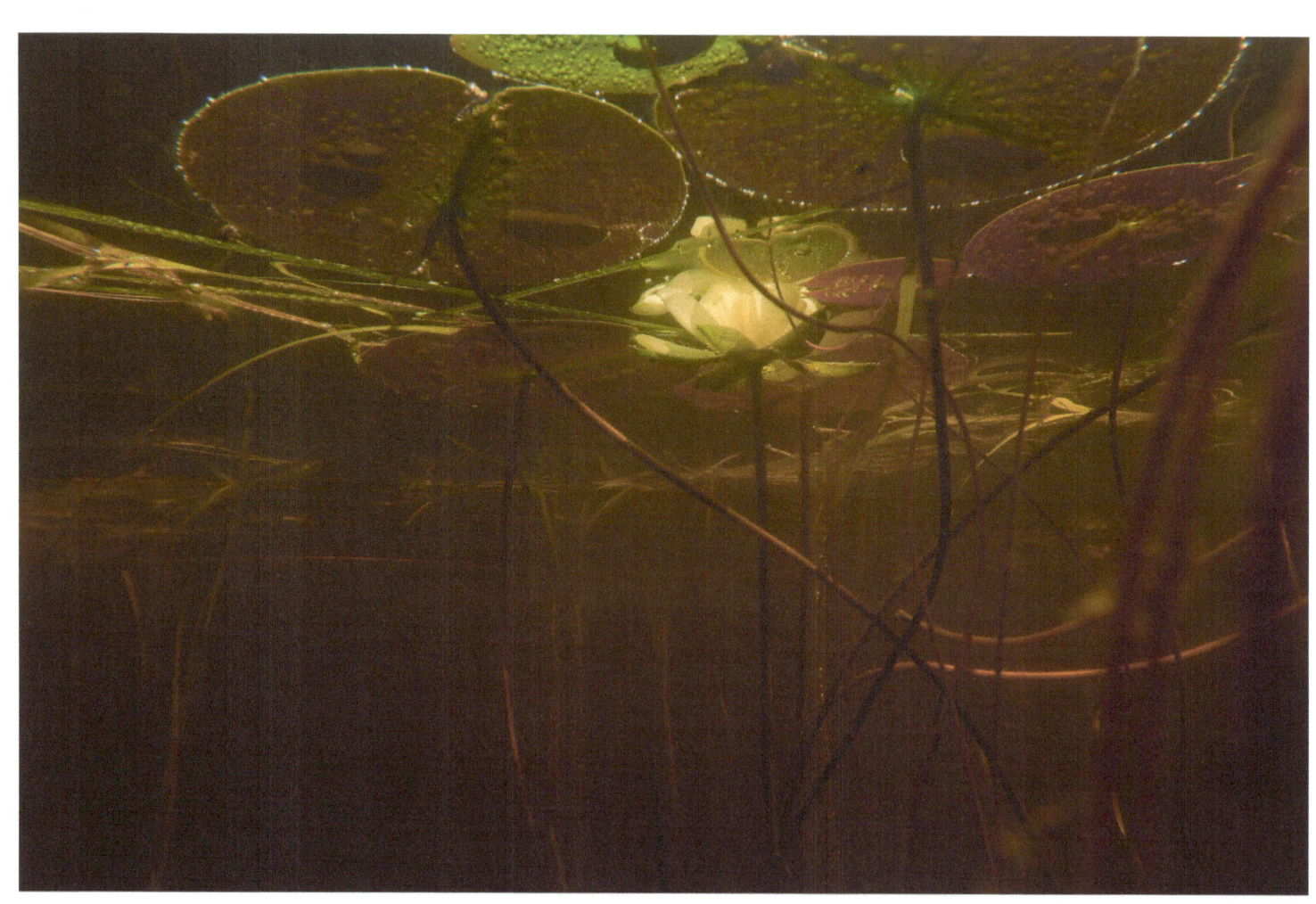

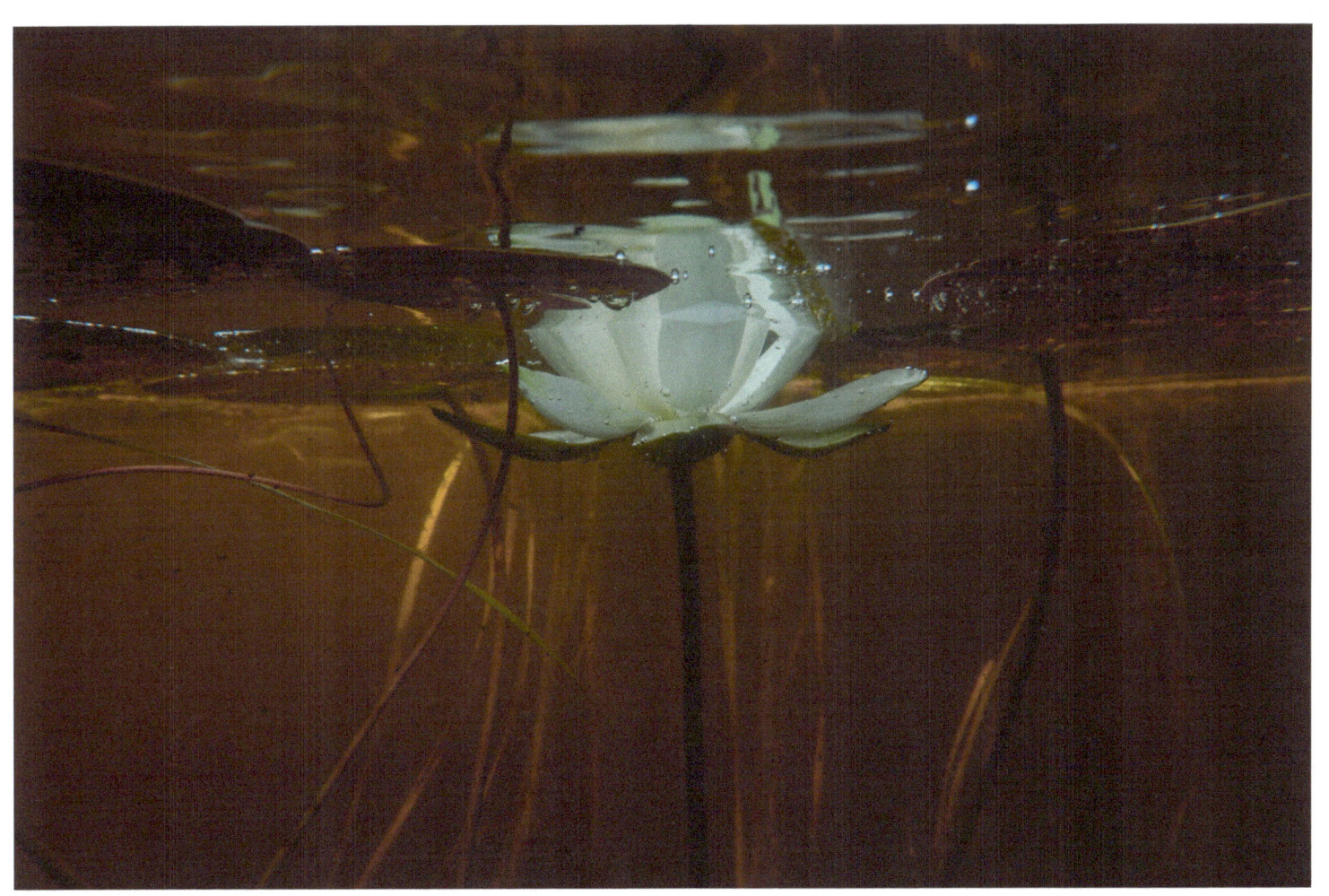

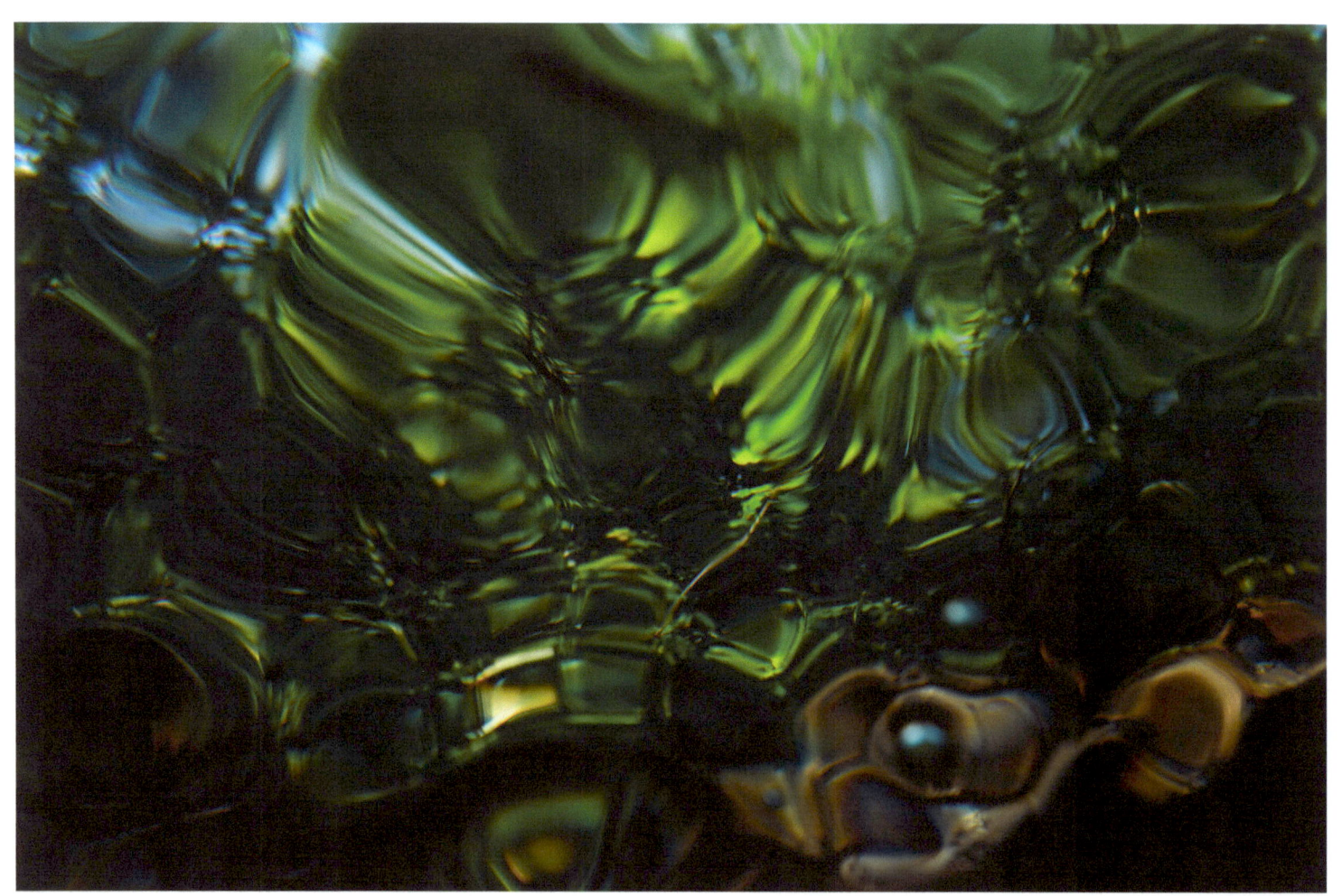

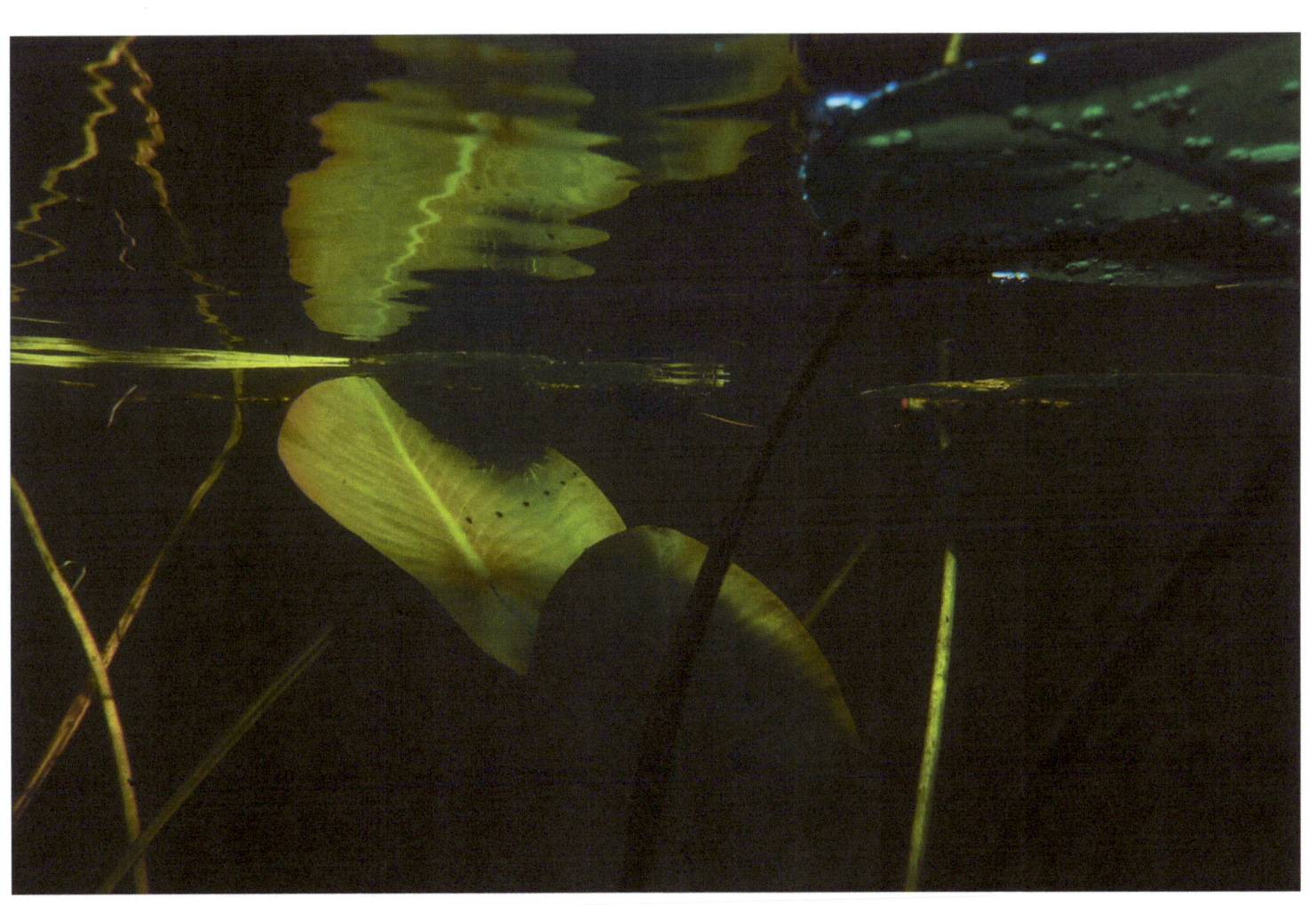

Return to the Surface

Rising again, flowers at the edge catch the sun, a solitary human pauses in reflection, and a fish glides through shallow water. The surface emerges not as a flat boundary but as a site of connection—between fragility and resilience, between the hidden and the seen. Having passed through both dark reds and luminous greens, the return to light carries a new awareness: the river is not only scenery but a living, complex system that sustains and mirrors life.

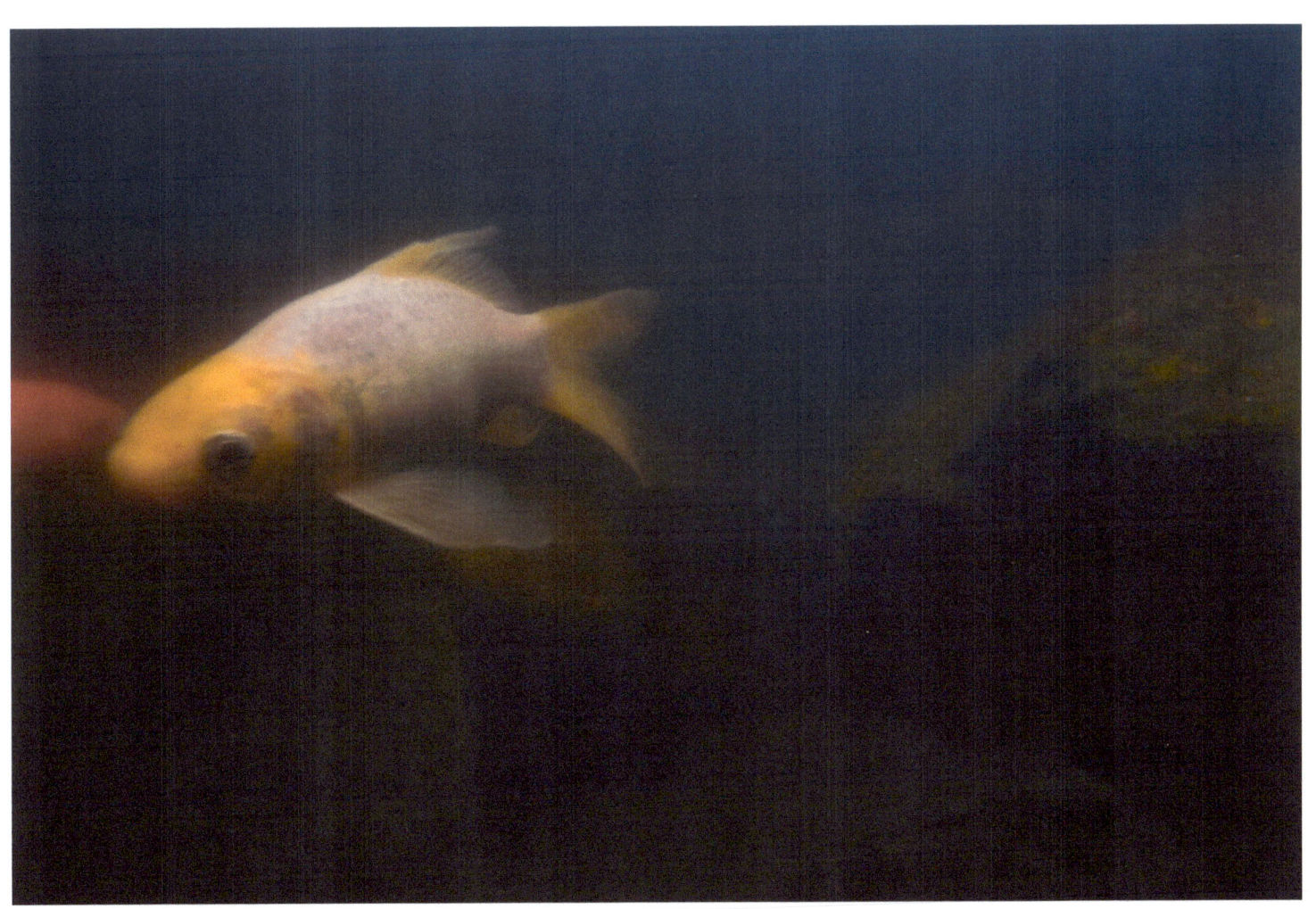

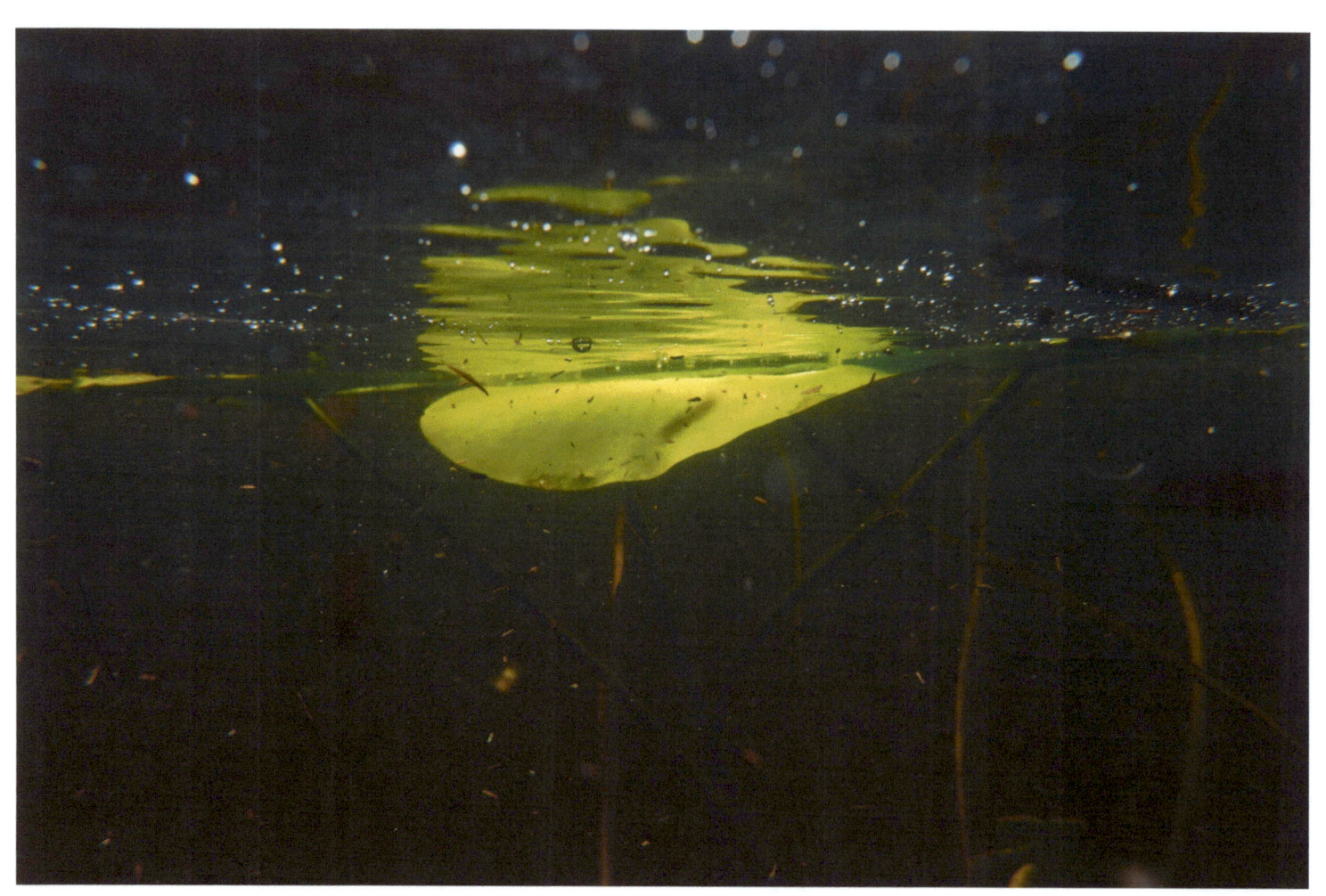

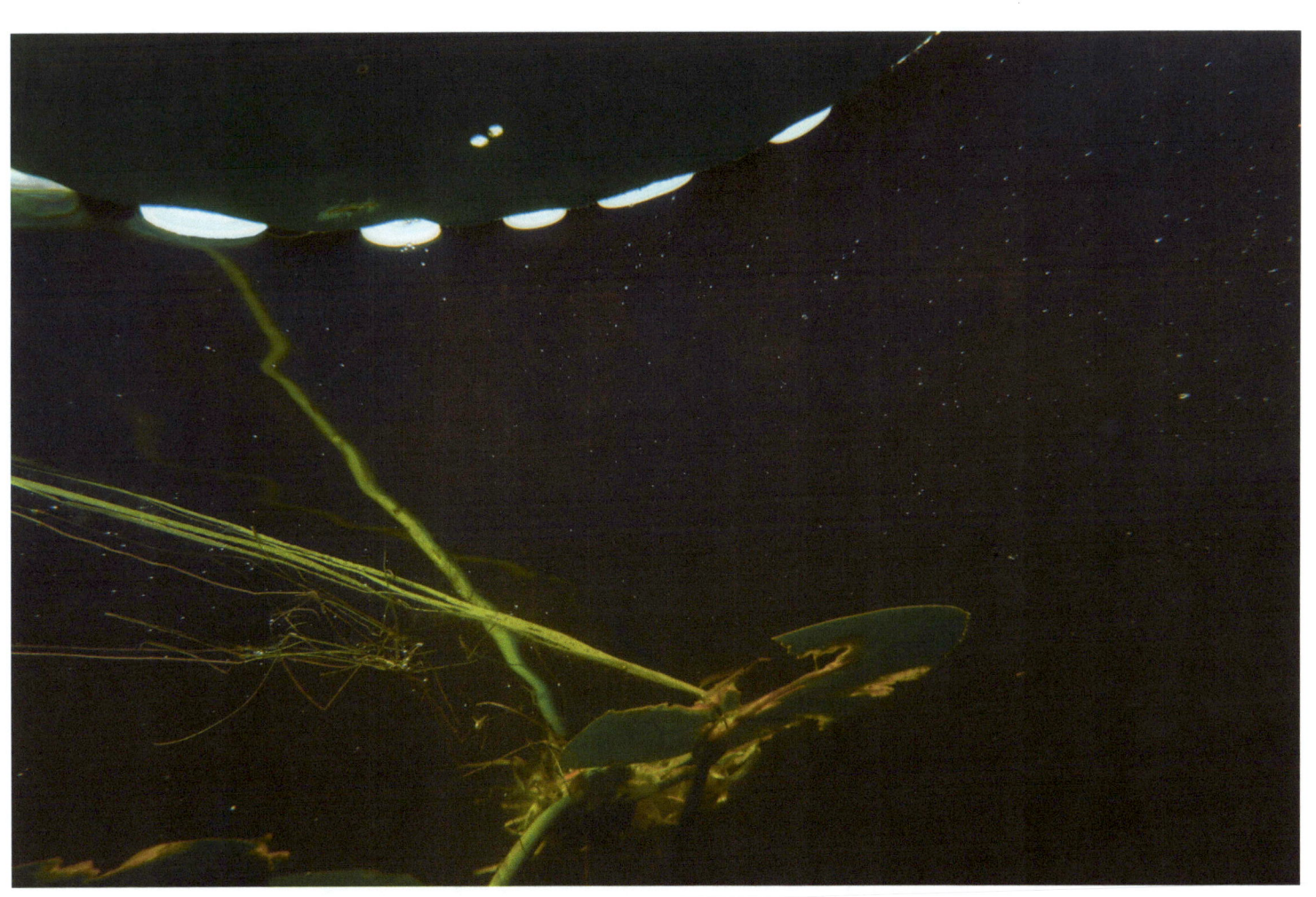

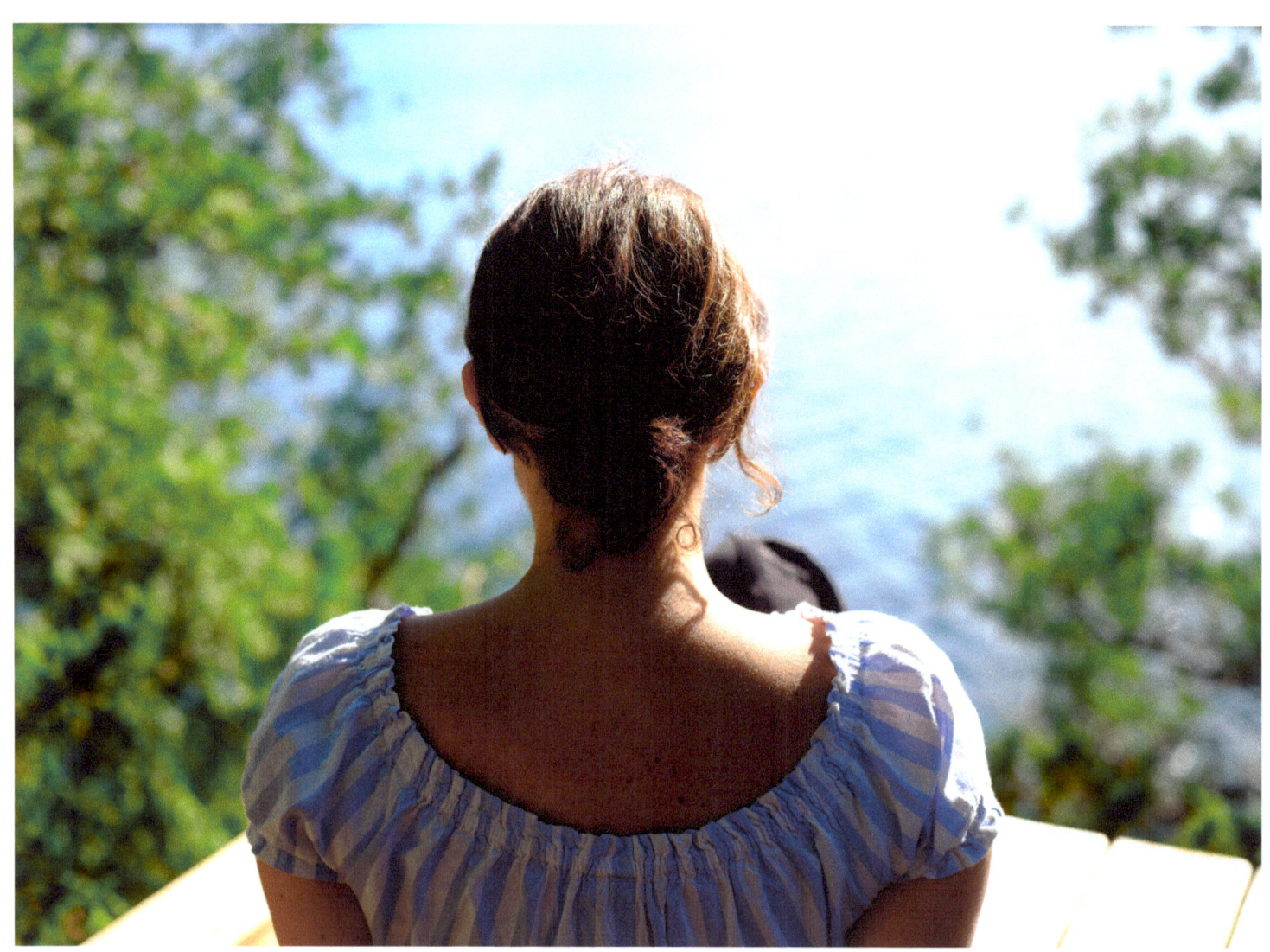

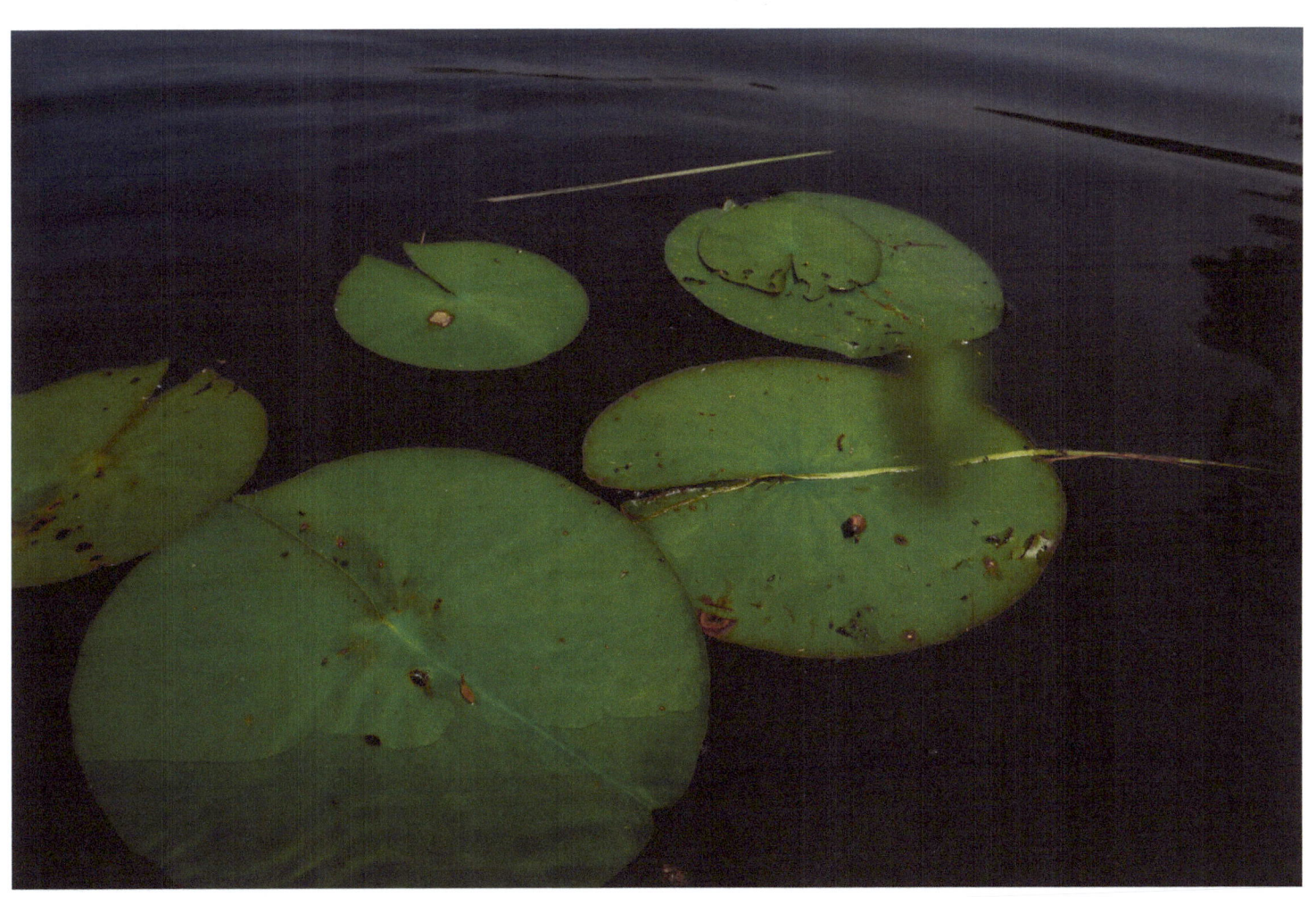

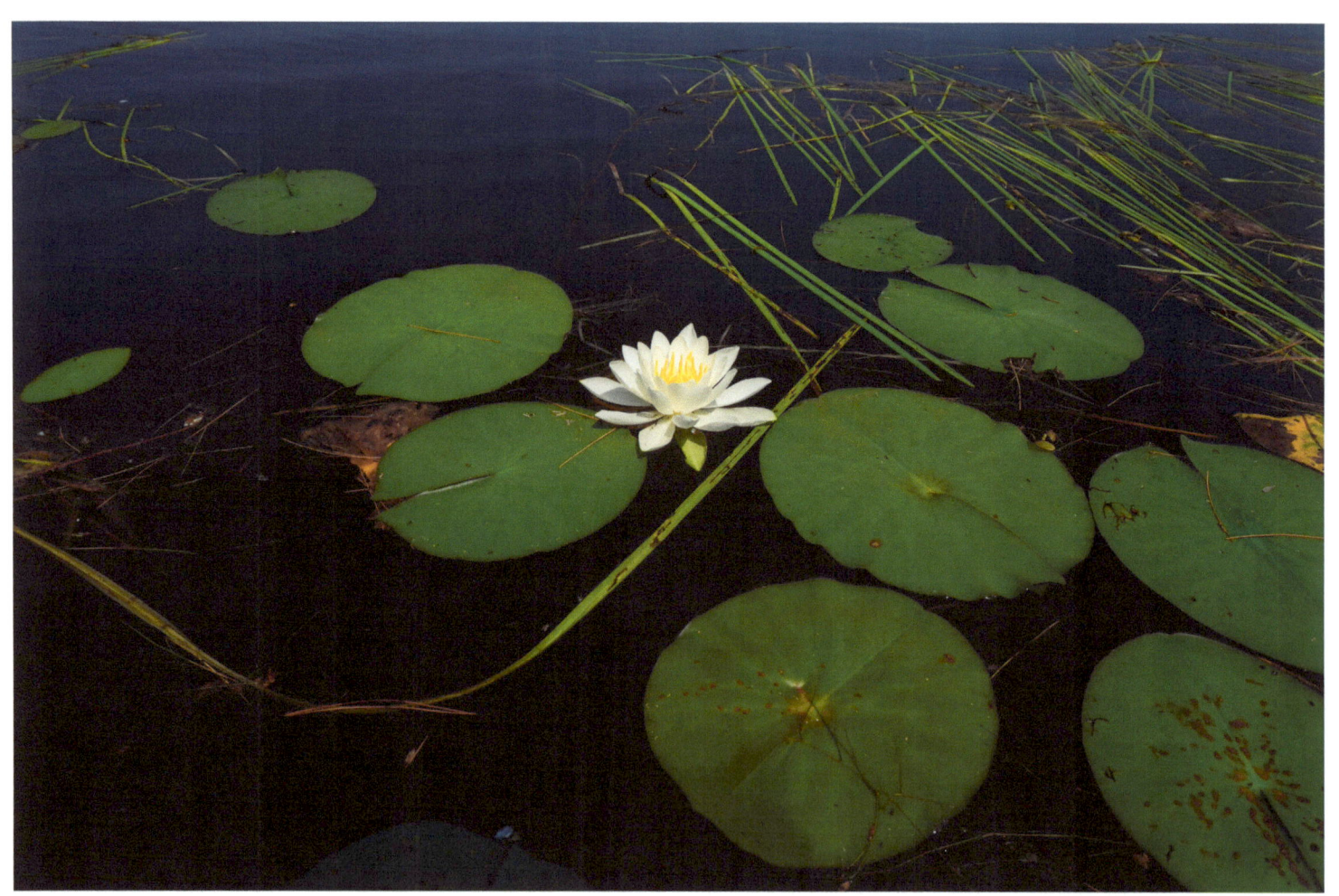

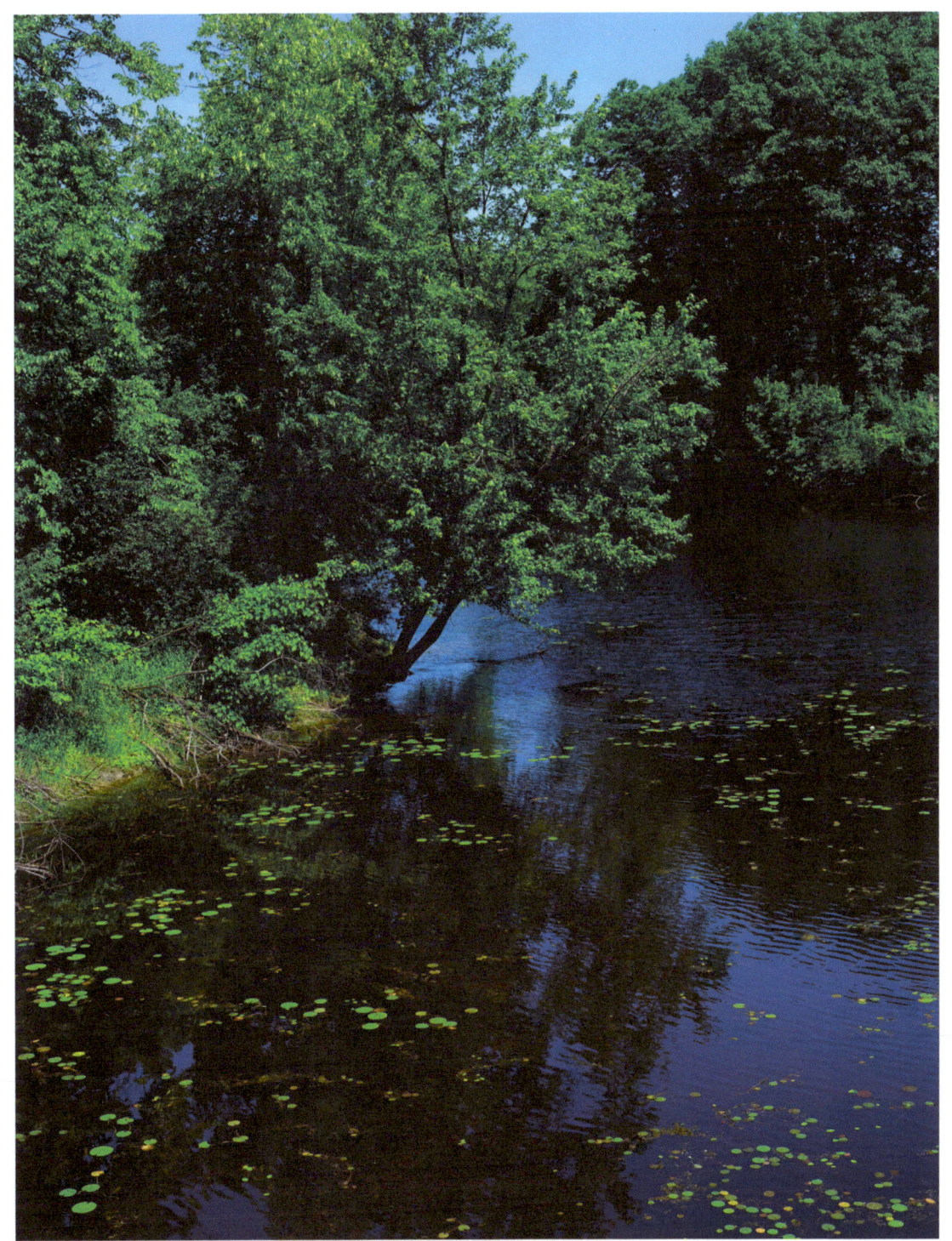

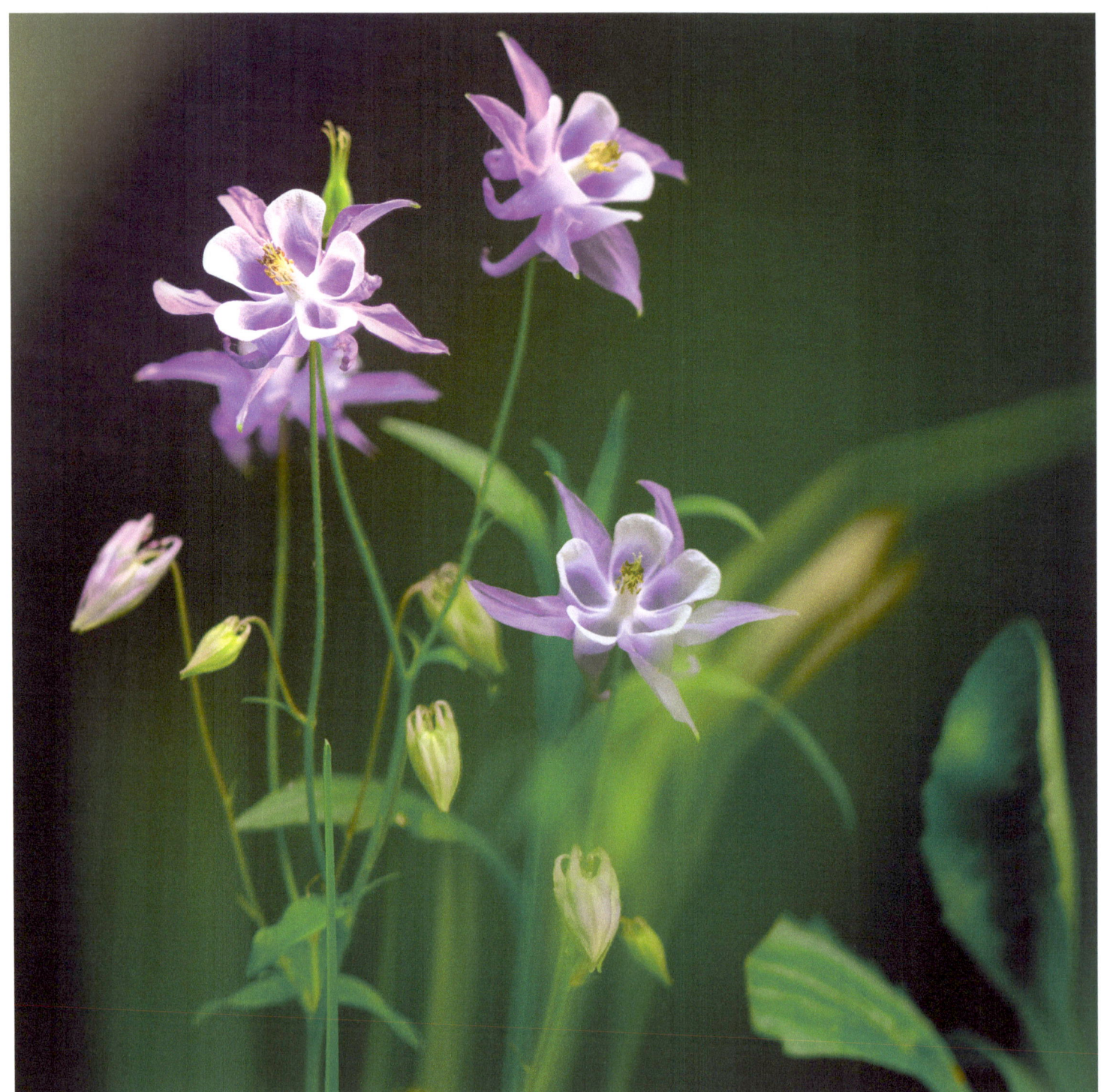

Imprints
(Cyanotypes)

In indigo depths, the river presses its memory into paper—a fragile trace and enduring mark at once. These cyanotypes embody both persistence and vulnerability, suggesting that what survives may be as much imprint as presence. They circle back to the central question: will these untouched worlds endure, or will memory be all that remains?

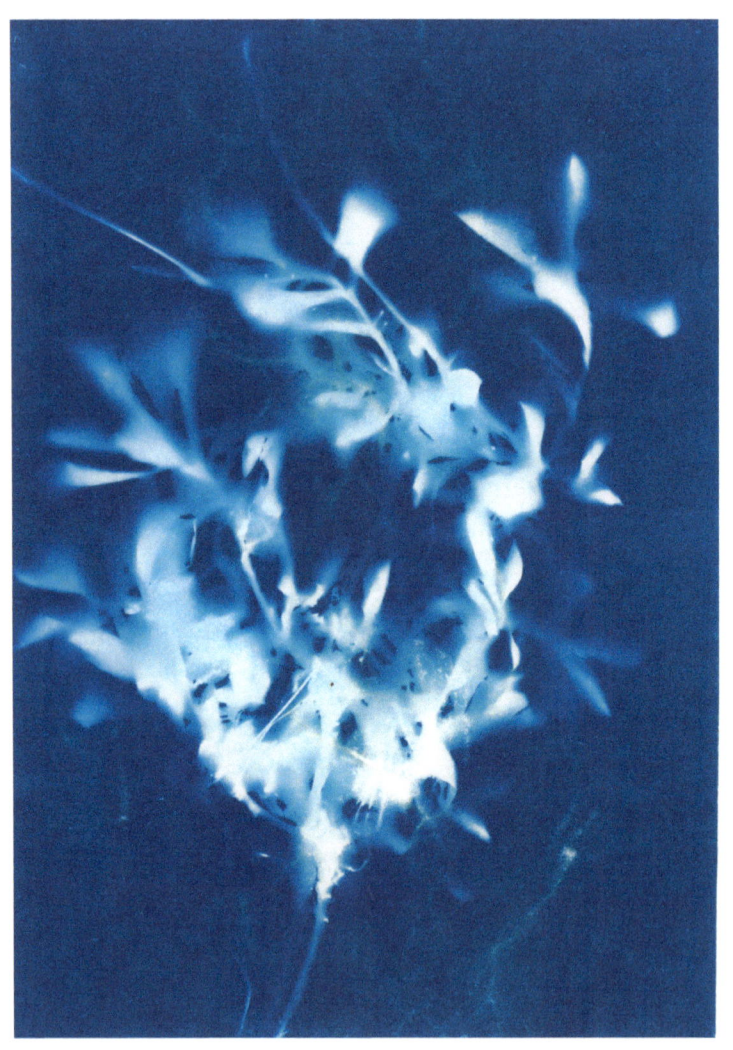
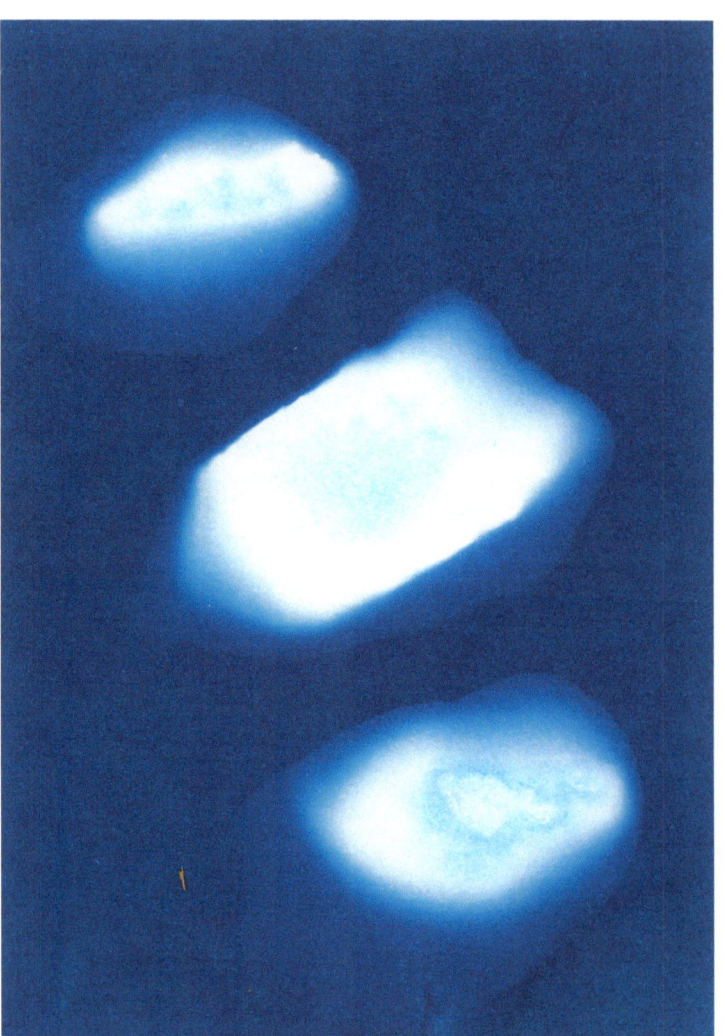

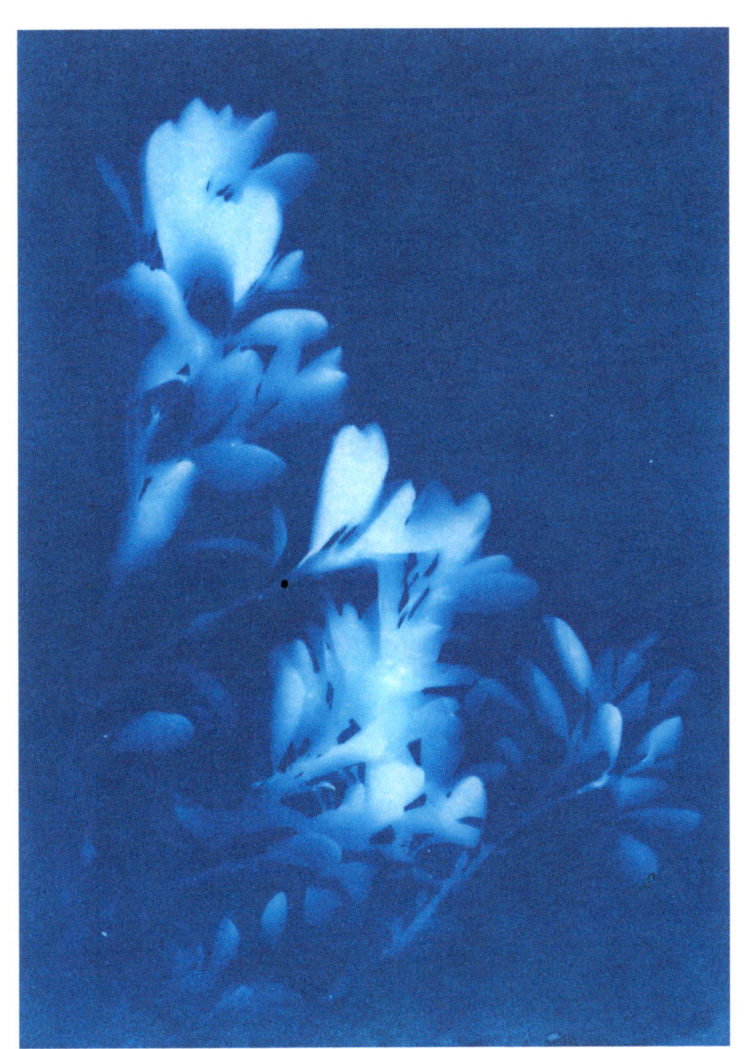 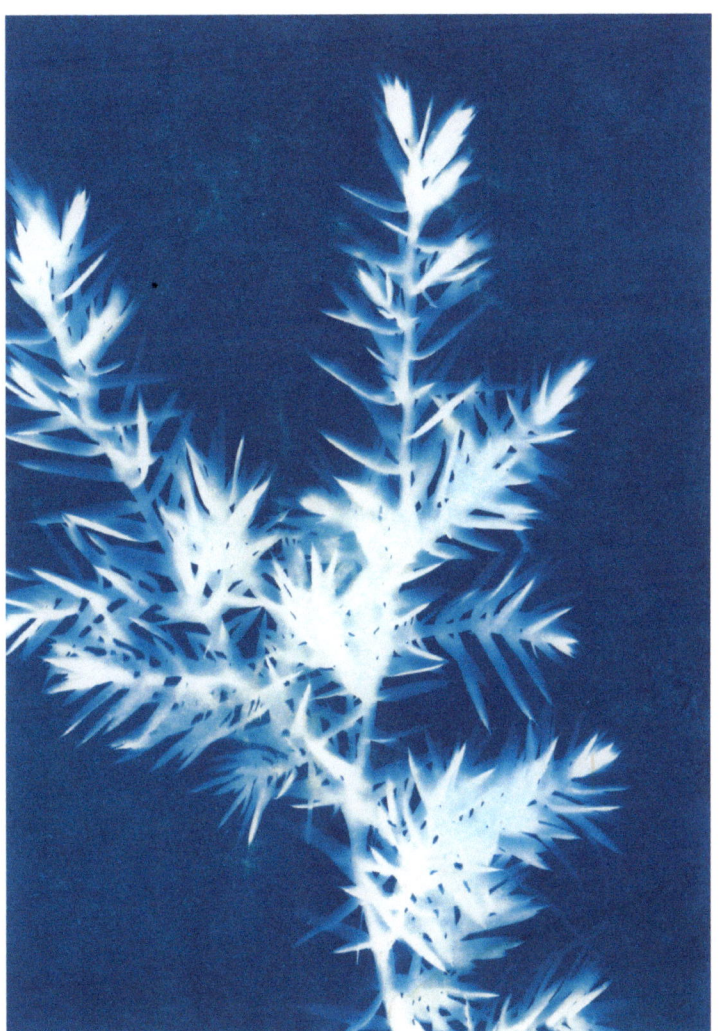

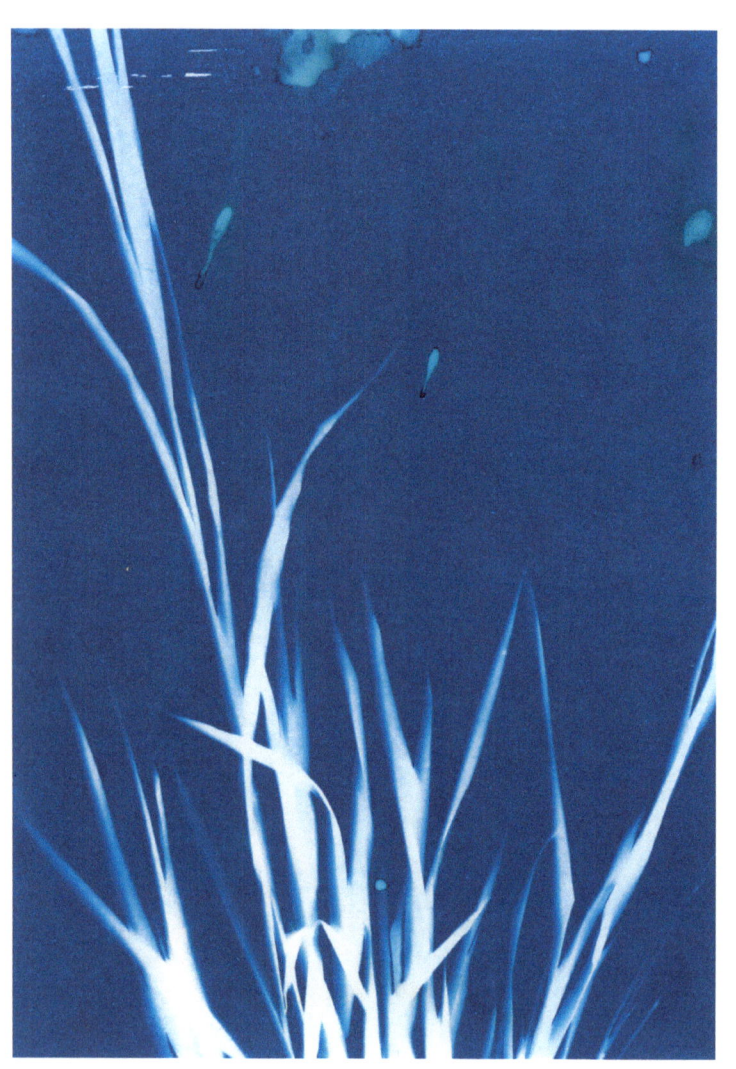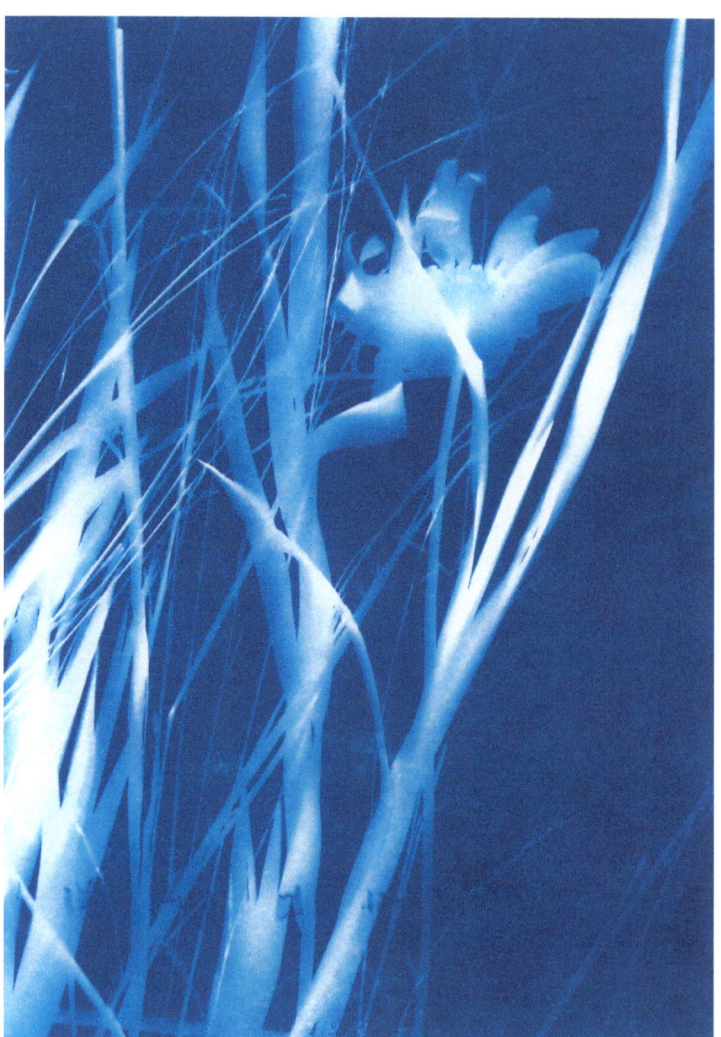

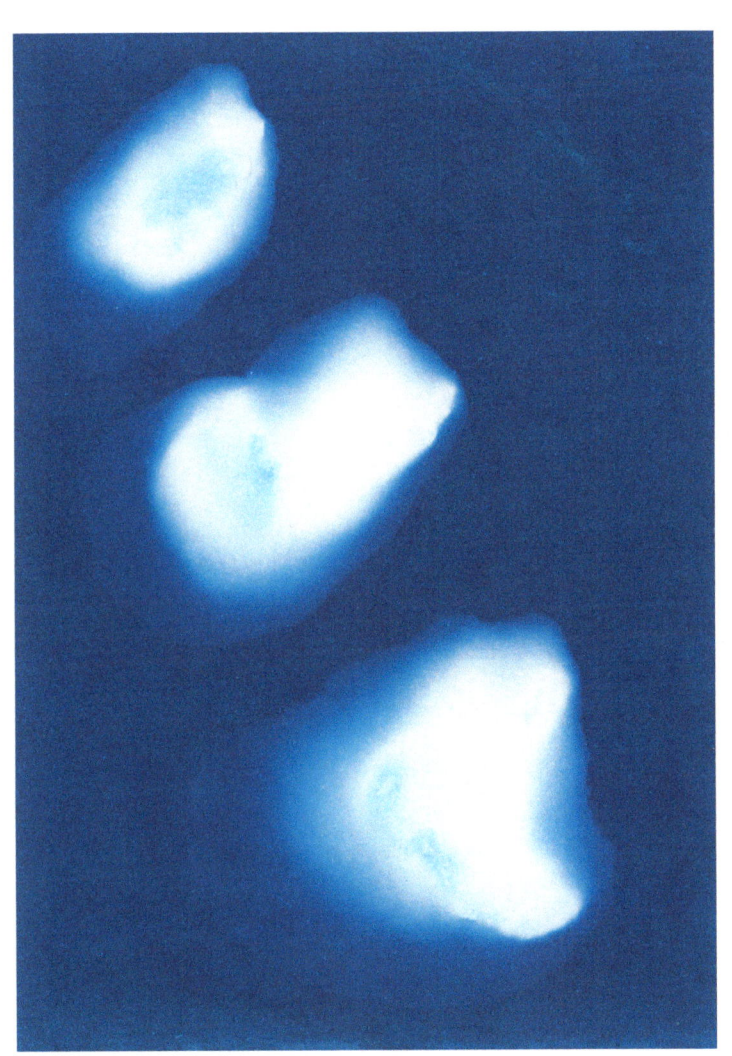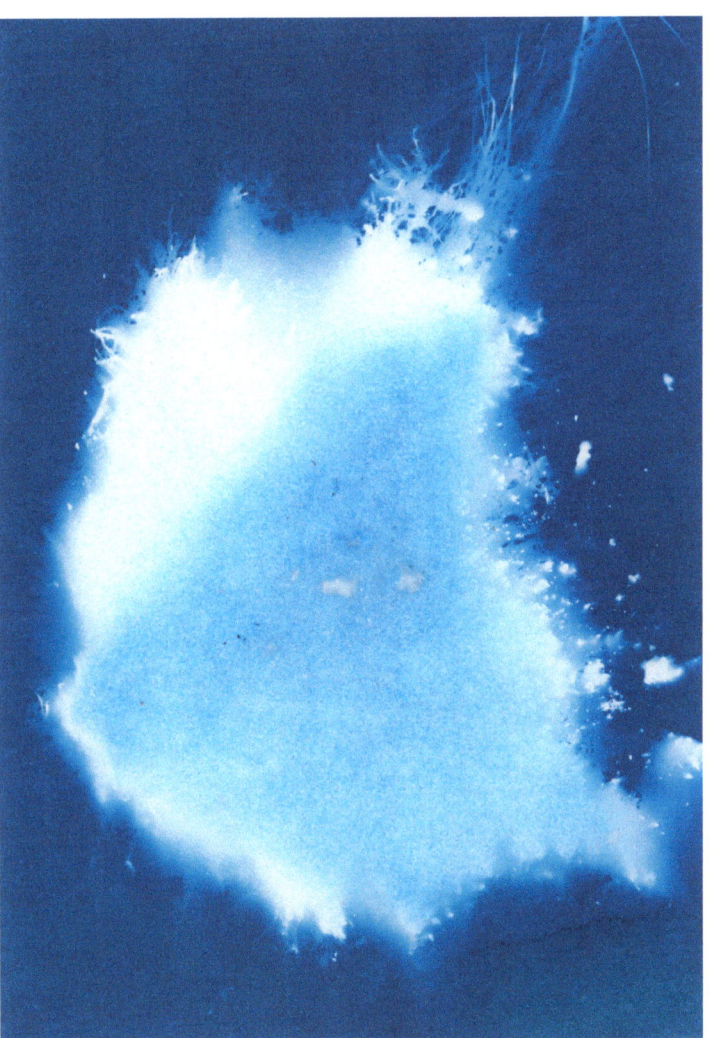

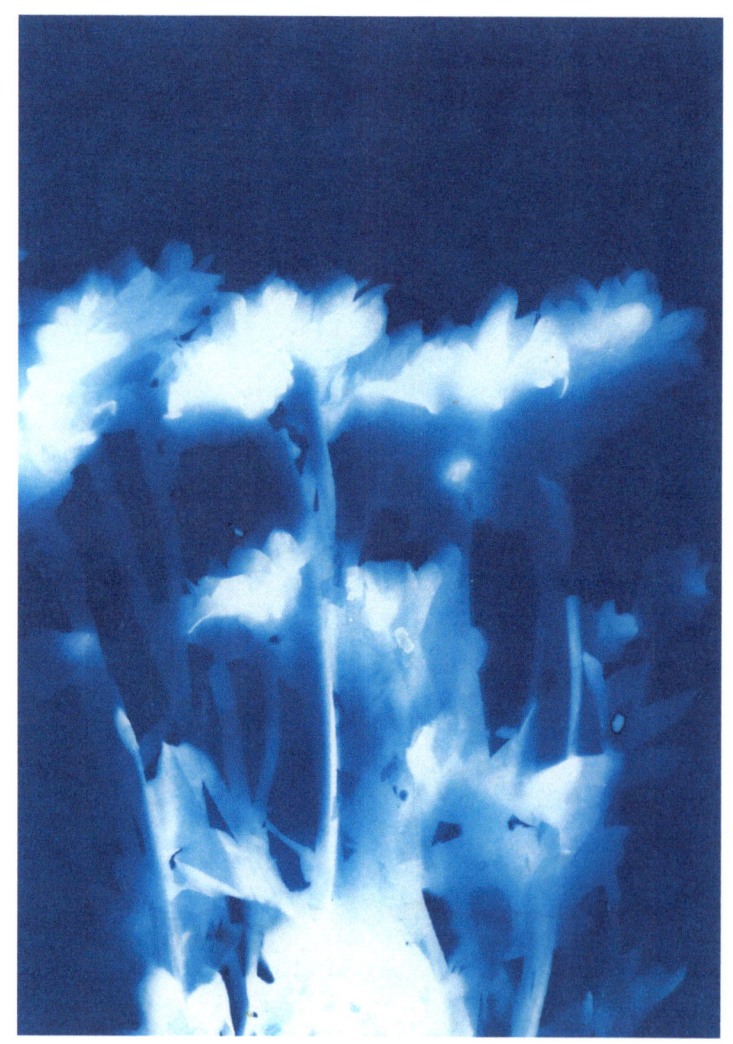

www.ingramcontent.com/pod-product-compliance
Lightning Source LLC
Chambersburg PA
CBHW040418220526
45473CB00004B/1279

MAGICAL, MYTHICAL, BEAUTIFUL & VERY REAL

UNICORNS

(A PHOTOBOOK FOR THOSE WHO BELIEVE)

P. GASSUS

No part of this publication may be reproduced, stored in a retrieval system, or transmitted in any form or by any means, electronic, mechanical, photocopying, recording, or otherwise, without written permission of the publisher.

For information regarding permission, or any other information write to info@moguldivision.com

Legal deposit, National Library of Canada, 2nd trimester, 2017
ISBN 978-1-987989-21-2

Copyright © 2017 Mogul Division Publishing
All rights reserved.

Published by Mogul Division Publishing
Printed in the U.S.A.